The Teacher
to Resea

This accessible guide provides practical support on becoming research-engaged and research active within the school and beyond. It explores the meaning of research and clarifies multiple types of research which lead to different views on 'what works', all whilst showing how to engage with the latest educational findings and how to conduct classroom-based research as part of career-long professional development.

Divided into three parts, this book uniquely discusses various understandings of being 'research-engaged' and covers key issues such as:

- Finding and interpreting research
- How to apply and evaluate findings in reliable ways
- Planning and carrying out a classroom-based project
- Building a culture of research within a school
- Establishing local research networks
- Publishing work

Illustrated with inspiring examples of how to implement these ideas in schools, *The Teacher's Guide to Research* is perfect for practicing school teachers, student teachers and educational leaders who are looking to expand their research knowledge and rekindle their professional curiosity. This deeper understanding of research will help empower teachers to shape the way pupils learn by investigating research ideas that work in a variety of contexts.

Jonathan Firth is a teacher, researcher and a Chartered Psychologist. He has written several school psychology textbooks as well as guides for teachers. He works in teacher education at the University of Strathclyde and teaches psychology at school level, as well as conducting research into the practical applications of memory and metacognition to teaching.

The Teacher's Guide to Research

Engaging with, Applying and Conducting Research in the Classroom

Jonathan Firth

Routledge
Taylor & Francis Group

LONDON AND NEW YORK

First published 2020
by Routledge
2 Park Square, Milton Park, Abingdon, Oxon OX14 4RN

and by Routledge
52 Vanderbilt Avenue, New York, NY 10017

Routledge is an imprint of the Taylor & Francis Group, an informa business

© 2020 Jonathan Firth

British Library Cataloguing-in-Publication Data
A catalogue record for this book is available from the British Library

Library of Congress Cataloging-in-Publication Data
A catalog record has been requested for this book

ISBN: 978-1-138-33625-4 (hbk)
ISBN: 978-1-138-33627-8 (pbk)
ISBN: 978-0-429-44312-1 (ebk)

Typeset in Galliard
by Swales & Willis, Exeter, Devon, UK

Contents

Contents

Introduction

Who is this book for?

This book is for and about teachers. It's primarily aimed at the classroom practitioner rather than managerial staff or other higher authorities. Why? Because in my view, engaging with research is a key part of teacher professionalism.[1] It is the teacher who enacts changes in the classroom, and by informing themselves about research, teachers can select and investigate ideas that make sense in their context.

Taking a research-informed approach to teaching is a matter of professional knowledge and skill, and potentially empowering. However, there's no doubt that some people have mixed feelings about this. 'Why do I need research', they might ask, 'when I already know how to teach?'. This question has led me to a careful consideration of how and why research engagement can be useful to the classroom teacher.

- If education is not informed by research, what is it informed by? All too often the answer will be traditions and assumptions, some of which will be flawed (and we won't even know which ones).

- Can a classroom teacher benefit from engaging with and taking part in research activities? In my view, the answer is yes—a research-engaged teacher has a deeper understanding of how learning works, and is in a better position to make changes to the benefit of pupils.

This book works through the process of informing yourself about research, using research, contributing to the research community, and sharing the outcomes of your research and conclusions with others as part of a broader movement.

How to engage with research

Engaging with research as a teacher does not necessarily mean that you have to conduct and publish your own research studies. It may be best, especially in the early stages, to focus more on understanding the work that has been done by others, as such evidence (especially that which is recent and high quality) will provide both a model of how to conduct research, and an introduction to current theories and debates. However, one of the best ways of engaging with any field of study is to participate in it, and there comes a point where you may wish to try things out for yourself, or attempt to answer questions that have not been satisfactorily dealt with in the research literature to date.

Answering questions and contributing to knowledge is not the only reason for conducting research in your classroom. It can also constitute an effective form of professional learning, being highly motivating and informative, and prompting professional reading and practical engagement with current issues.

How can teachers take control of their development?

To say that teachers can and should be evidence informed is a challenging statement, and one which suggests a shift in the nature of the role. Research can be an empowering process, allowing a teacher to change aspects of their practice on the basis of evidence. However, in order to be empowering, the teacher must remain the decision maker. A fundamental dilemma in the education system as a whole is that while governments and other external bodies want to improve teacher professionalism, doing so in a top-down way—where teachers are told what to do and how to do it—is fundamentally disempowering, and therefore harmful to the processes as a whole.[2] So one initial principle is that in order for evidence-based practice to work, the teacher needs to at least have a role in setting the research agenda, and needs to be able to act on the outcome of the research. If neither of these principles hold, then teacher research engagement is reduced to a hollow, tick-box exercise.

What about research that does not study learning?

Although the emphasis in this book is on research which can directly affect your teaching practice (with such work often termed action research or practitioner enquiry), there is no reason that teachers need to be limited to researching issues of teaching and learning. There is an entire chapter (Chapter 13) on research within your subject discipline, which also includes guidance on encouraging and supporting pupil-led research projects.

How this book is structured

Each chapter covers a key aspect of research engagement, in an order which moves from information (for example, how to find and read journal articles), via increasingly elaborate practical engagement, and finally on to sharing research and establishing research systems in your school.

Each chapter also explores an educational case study, includes a summary of a key issue from the research literature, discussion points for staff reading groups, and a suggestion for a practical project.

Later in the book, you will also find a glossary of terms.

There are three main parts in the book:

Part 1: Research for the teacher

This part looks at how and why teachers access research, overcoming barriers including the issue of finding enough time, and explores how to find, apply and evaluate research-informed changes to practice.

It answers some of the big questions about engaging with research: why, when, what, who and how:

Why: Chapter 1, why teachers should engage with research.
When: Chapter 2, finding the time for research.
What: Chapter 3, accessing and using research evidence.
Who: Chapter 4, will this work for my learners?
How: Chapter 5, using a research-based intervention in your classroom, and Chapter 6, evaluating your intervention.

Part 2: The teacher as researcher

This part describes how to ensure that teacher-led research projects are ethical and valid, and sets out the various methodology options available for running your own full-scale research study.

Ethical practice and an understanding of ethics is relevant at any point, but it seemed to make sense to place the ethics chapter before the chapters on data gathering and running research studies. Having said this, as a research-engaged teacher you would benefit from reading this chapter at any point in the process.

Part 3: The networked teacher-researcher

This part focuses on the systems and networks that can support a teacher who is becoming research-engaged, including the establishment of research centres in schools, local groups and issues around sharing and disseminating research.

About the author

Jonathan Firth is a teacher, researcher and a Chartered Psychologist. He has written several school psychology textbooks as well as guides for teachers. He works in teacher education at the University of Strathclyde and teaches psychology at school level, as well as conducting research into the practical applications of memory and metacognition to teaching.

Notes

1 Firth, J. (2017). Experts in learning. In L. Rycroft-Smith & J. L. Dutaut (Eds.) *Flip the system UK: A teachers' manifesto* (pp. 20–28). Abingdon, UK: Routledge.
2 Sachs, J. (2016). Teacher professionalism: why are we still talking about it? *Teachers and Teaching*, 22(4), 413–425.

PART 1
Research for the teacher

This part looks at the practical issues involved in engaging with research. We consider why it should be done at all as part of your professional practice (Chapter 1), and how to make time for it (Chapter 2). We then move on to the skills involved in accessing research evidence and applying interventions based on this evidence (Chapters 3–5), and then consider how to evaluate, in an unbiased way, whether a change has actually been beneficial (Chapter 6).

This part is, therefore, very much focused on learning about and using *existing* research. The later two parts ('the teacher as researcher' and 'the networked teacher-researcher') look at issues around conducting and disseminating research of your own.

Why teachers should engage with research

Throughout school learning, we aim for our pupils to be inspired, curious and questioning. We also expect the curriculum of school education to be based on facts, derived from a sound and reliable body of scientific evidence and wisdom, not the opinions of the few, or the fashions of the day.

It is strange, therefore, how different the picture is when it comes to research and its relationship with classroom practice—engaging with research is not typically seen as a part of the teacher's role.[1] Before we get into the issue of when and how to engage with research (Chapters 2–6), let's first consider why we might wish to do it in the first place.

Responding to events

The classroom is not a predictable place. Teaching and sitting exams is sometimes unfavourably compared to a factory process, but as every teacher knows, there are far too many unpredictable events—from behaviour to pupil responses to interruptions—for it to be possible to plan or script everything to the letter. Teaching is, therefore, a process that requires a high level of decision making and a fair amount of improvisation.

In both the lesson planning stage, the lesson itself, and the aftermath (feedback, review, further planning), a teacher therefore has to make judgement calls about what to do and when to do it. Should a learner be given feedback now, or later or not at all? Should we reward successful work? Should the class work individually or in pairs?

It could be argued that there are two main sources of information when making these decisions:

- Experience. Experienced teachers make better decisions than novices, in part because they have made many mistakes in the past, and are able to avoid similar mistakes in the future by changing their own actions.

- Research. Research evidence can tell us what has been done in other comparable circumstances and what the outcome was.

These two sources of information can and should both feed into the teacher's professional decision-making process. Realistically, research cannot replace experience—if it could, then it would be possible to train the perfect teacher simply by exposing them to theory and research evidence.

Likewise however, experience cannot entirely replace evidence. If it could, then research wouldn't actually be necessary! If any call could be made just by drawing on experience, then we could simply ask experienced teachers what to do. Unfortunately, reality shows us that even very experienced teachers harbour misconceptions about how learning and behaviour work, and that the outcome of research is often surprising and counterintuitive (see discussion on pp. 11–13).

Should you review this topic now, or tomorrow or in a month's time? Should you mark this essay with detailed comments, or ask the pupils to peer mark? Should you use real-world examples and let pupils figure out the rules, or present ideas more theoretically? For these and hundreds of other decisions, research can point the way in areas where our intuitive sense of what's effective can let us down. Research can guide us towards choices which lead to better learning—learning that pupils retain over the long term and are able to **transfer** to multiple situations throughout life. It can also help us to improve pupil engagement, and save time by weeding out ineffective practices.

Just as with other professions, then, such as medicine or engineering, our professional experience can be (and arguably should be) enhanced by engaging with research findings from science or social science. This allows the professional to make *informed* decisions. In this book, we will explore how research engagement can complement, not replace, other aspects of a teacher's professionalism.

Misconceptions and the role of evidence

Some situations within a teacher's role are fairly easy to judge simply on the basis of intuition and common sense: we can all see whether a pupil is upset, for example, and a lack of motivation is usually clearly evident too.

However, as noted above, education is subject to many misconceptions, and some aspects of human thinking and learning are not intuitive (see From the research on p. 11). Creativity is a good example—it's not immediately obvious what processes will lead to someone having a worthwhile creative idea. Some aspect of learning are similarly hard to judge; pupils can leave the classroom confident that they have learned, and the teacher may also be confident if the class have successfully completed a quiz or exit pass at the end of the session. But what about forgetting? If the key information is forgotten within a few hours or weeks, it doesn't seem reasonable to say that it has been learned, even if performance was very good in the short term. Some researchers into memory have drawn a distinction between performance and learning. It may only be possible to infer learning by testing pupils after a delay, and doing so shows that forgetting has a much greater and faster impact than tends to be anticipated.

This raises a broader issue—are the views of teachers and their pupils subject to misconceptions about how learning works, and if so, can we trust 'common sense' approaches to the learning process, and how do these relate to the role of research evidence?

From the research

Key issue: is teaching mainly a matter of common sense? Teachers may feel that they can rely on their gut feeling, particularly after they have accumulated many years of classroom experience. Perhaps, in fact, teaching is more of an art than a science. But at

(continued)

(continued)

times, our gut feeling may conflict with the scientific evidence on a topic. So which is more reliable?

What the research says: teaching is a highly complex skill. It is one of the most demanding of all professions, because it involves not just dealing with human beings (which are always more complex than physical objects) but modifying something intangible—the formation of new memories. Understandably, then, there are areas where research will highlight issues that conflict with cultural norms and 'common sense' practices.

Does this mean that all research will show mainstream teaching practice to be wrong? Not at all. Some research will confirm what you thought already, and this is to be welcomed—it would be strange and disturbing if we found out that teachers were getting every single thing wrong! However, when research papers do tell us that common classroom practices are ineffective or inefficient, this is also to be welcomed because it points the way towards improvements that can be made. Research findings may present alternatives that are easier to do, or lead to a more lasting impact.

Cognitive psychologists Robert and Elizabeth Bjork and colleagues have studied a number of counterintuitive findings in education. Among other things, they have shown that reducing the frequency and amount of feedback results in more errors in the short term, but better learning in the long term.[2] In addition, waiting a couple of weeks before consolidation rather than doing it soon after a lesson runs counter to standard teaching practice, but research on the spacing effect suggests that doing so is beneficial (at least in *most* circumstances—more on adapting these findings to your own classroom in Chapter 4).

Together, these findings have been described as **desirable difficulties**. They are features of the learning situation that appear to make learning harder and more error-prone (in other words, they harm performance) and are therefore usually avoided by learners and teachers alike, but which lead to more durable learning in the long run. Understanding these areas can help teachers to cut out ineffective practices, and can also help sound practices to be used in the right way and in the right context.

What exactly do we mean by 'evidence'?

From what has been said so far, evidence can be seen as fundamental to improving education. For changes to be made, they need to be based on sound, unbiased research evidence, and account for some of the limited ideas which can result from over-reliance on intuition.

But what exactly is evidence? It can take many forms. Later chapters in this book will compare some of the different research methods that can be used within education, some of which you may choose to try out for yourself. For now, suffice to say that there are many ways of gathering evidence, and all have their flaws. It certainly shouldn't be assumed that the term only applies to large-scale studies such as randomised controlled trials (RCTs). Your notes from talking to a parent is a form of evidence, as is your class's work, their test scores and anything else that provides information about their progress. All of these forms of evidence could influence our decision-making process.

Published research evidence is based on one or more context—contexts that differ from your own. While this can be a flaw, such work is also more likely to illuminate general principles. For example, a study that looks at motivation over several different primary classes might help us to understand how motivation works in general terms, not just what one of your learners or their dad thinks about the current reading book.

Even though such evidence cannot override the specifics of our classes and their needs or our professional or ethical judgement, they can add another dimension to it, ensuring that any choices are research-based as well as being informed by our own experiences.

Viewing evidence in this way can fundamentally change how we see teacher professionalism. Teachers are all too often placed in a situation where they are told what good practice looks like, and then observed to ensure that this is what they are doing—a 'top-down' approach to research that leads to stress, not research engagement.[3] Instead, this book advocates becoming actively and autonomously research engaged, so that teachers find themselves in the position of making these educational judgements for themselves while still working within school priorities and policies. What's more, rather than the generic advice that teaching authorities and governments can give, teachers can combine an understanding of evidence with their professional knowledge of their learners. This puts them in the best position to be the decision makers in education.[4]

The research-engaged teacher may go through a process of reading and discussing the research, prior to starting to implement it. This implementation might be tentative at first, but as time goes on and some early changes start to pay off, new research-informed changes may start to flow with more confidence and spontaneity.

As a teacher, one of the best feelings you can have comes from the professional empowerment of autonomously making a research-informed change and seeing it benefit your learners. In contrast, there are few feelings worse than having bad practices foisted upon you, or simply blundering about in the dark, unsure whether what you are doing is effective or not!

Teachers can therefore be seen as consumers of research, and this can be the beginning of a longer process too. As time goes on, taking existing evidence on board might not be enough. You could also act as a producer of research which other teachers will view and respond to, or as a stakeholder who sets the research agenda together with others such as university academics or government agencies. As Graham Donaldson, education advisor to the Scottish and Welsh governments, has said:

> There is an urgent need to challenge the narrow interpretations of the teacher's role which have created unhelpful philosophical and structural divides, and have led to sharp separations of function amongst teachers, teacher educators and researchers.
>
> Donaldson, 2011 (p. 5)

Case study: priming pupils for learning

This case study focuses on Ashley, a secondary science teacher who has been working mainly with Year 7–11 classes:

> Ashley has always assumed that learners, particularly young learners, are like empty vessels, ready to be filled with knowledge. As such, she hasn't paid much attention to their prior knowledge, other than to assume a basic general knowledge such as familiarity with parts of the world and common animals.
>
> Recently, however, Ashley has been reading about how memories are structured in long-term memory, and about the importance of making links with existing knowledge. She has begun to realise that it would be valuable to focus more on their existing knowledge and prior assumptions.
>
> In order to do this, Ashley gives her Year 7 class a short quiz about animals, prior to beginning a new topic on wildlife and habitats. She includes several questions that will be covered during the topic itself, and which she would not expect pupils to be able to answer correctly. Responses to these questions are then used in a short group discussion task, before Ashley begins her explanation.
>
> As this task progresses, two things happen. One is that Ashley realises that many of her learners knew more than she had realised at the start of the topic. The other is that when she begins her explanation of the topic content, the learners show considerably more curiosity than is usually the case, reacting with enthusiasm when they find out answers to questions that had previously confused them.

Ashley's case is a good example of how reading about the science of learning can prompt a teacher to reevaluate their

(continued)

(continued)

assumptions, and make modifications to practice. It also shows that starting to be evidence informed doesn't mean rejecting all aspects of a existing practice, and can proceed gradually, one idea or activity at a time.

The case also links to the **pre-testing effect**—a finding in cognitive science which shows that asking learners questions before a lesson, even if they are unable to answer, can boost attention and lead to better retention of the new information.

Gaining a general background

As a teacher who is beginning to engage (or re-engage) with research, it is very tempting to read about one or two recent findings and immediately begin to make changes that you hope will improve outcomes for learners.

However, it can be difficult to fully appreciate the implications of research literature without first establishing a broader, more foundational knowledge. Among our pupils, we would not advise reading complex research papers before learning about the subject in general, with a conceptual understanding and familiarity with key terms already firmly in place. It is very similar for the teacher who engages with research.

Areas of education, as with other social sciences, also tend to bleed into one another—for example, it's difficult to fully tackle issues of reading difficulties on a cognitive level without also considering the role of social class and identity.[5]

University-based researchers tend to specialise in a small number of areas and may lack familiarity of other areas, but teachers need a more general grounding for practical reasons—we can't choose to ignore key aspects of classroom practice like motivation or feedback! David Weston of the Teacher Development Trust has compared school teachers to general practitioners in the world of medicine—we require a bit of everything in terms of research knowledge, and don't have the luxury of skipping entire areas. It's a good analogy; teachers do need a broad grounding, but this doesn't mean that they can't also have one or more specialist interests where they engage in practical research, or even publish. After all, many GPs do so.

Ideally, teachers will have gained a sound theory-based background of issues such as learning and behaviour during their initial teacher preparation (using this term fairly broadly, to refer to the multiple ways of training or educating new teachers). But there's a limit to how much a new teacher can be expected to take on board without a grounding in classroom experiences to which to link their new learning. To draw an analogy with Ashley's science learners (see the case study on p. 15), the new teacher will take in theoretical information better if it can be linked to experience and background knowledge.

As time goes on, a teacher's level of both experience and theoretical understanding will increase, leading to a (hopefully) virtuous cycle through which each benefits the other. Such a state can only be achieved with sustained professional reading of research alongside classroom practice. Some teachers might go on to undertake further formal education, such as a postgraduate qualification which focuses on an in-depth understanding of social science concepts relevant to education. However in the shorter term, the study of subjects such as psychology, sociology and neuroscience would provide an excellent grounding into key concepts in education, as well as how these fit into broader theoretical frameworks.

Consider the following points:

- How much do you and your colleagues know about the basics of psychology?
- Will it be a barrier for your team to study research into education without this background knowledge?
- How could a teacher improve their broad general knowledge of this subject?

General textbooks are a great starting point for your research engagement, simply because of the need to establish a broad knowledge base in your professional learning.

However, it's important to remember that many of the ideas that appear in general textbooks are somewhat outdated, and are included because of their historical importance to the field rather than because current researchers actually subscribe to them.

A good example of this is the 'modal model' of memory—the theory that shows memory as divided into three key stores: sensory memory, short-term memory and long-term memory. The modal model was devised over 50 years ago, in the very early days of cognitive psychology. Psychologists now understand that short-term memory (usually now referred to as *working memory*) and long-term memory each have different parts or sub-stores. Therefore it's important to recognise the context of information from textbooks—historical importance is often prioritised, and textbooks typically provide a primer rather than delving into research debates in detail.

Research project: a useful introduction to the role of evidence in education would be to investigate the different types of evidence that a teacher could potentially use. For this task, you will compare the relative benefits of published research and data gathered through your own classroom processes.

How to do it: firstly, think of a teaching relevant area that could be studied, for example, motivation. Now list all of the ways that you could gather evidence about a class's motivation. For example, surveys, observations, research studies about motivation, and so on. Next, think of at least three forms of evidence which could be usefully triangulated to provide different perspectives on the same educational issue.

Special note: for any data gathering involved in the projects throughout this book, ethical procedures must be followed. The projects in Chapters 1–7 do not involve primary data gathering, but please refer to Chapter 8, 'Ethics' (in Part 2 of this book) if you do intend to gather data beyond what is normally gathered in the course of carrying out your teaching role.

Concluding comments

We are witnessing a movement from myth to science in education. No longer is good teaching practice seen as a matter of tradition. Instead, any aspect of effective teaching and learning is open to scrutiny. What actually gets results? What side effects might a change have? What ends are we trying to achieve? Engaging with these questions will be part of teacher professionalism in the decades to come.

Many of the ideas throughout this book will make teaching easier and reduce stress. Learning is likely to be more successful if it is informed by evidence, and this means that more will get done in the same amount of time. This leads to better results—keeping learners happy, and cutting the stress level for teachers, too. Higher achieving, more motivated and resilient learners are easier and more pleasant to teach. When learners understand their own learning processes, are highly motivated and work well independently, this again reduces workload.

A deep understanding of classroom processes is important to the profession. Deep, research-based knowledge about learning is one of the key things that sets a professional teacher apart from a student helper or classroom volunteer, and is what puts the teacher in the position to make high-stakes choices about their learners and about the curriculum. Concurrently, there is personal satisfaction and a confidence boost to be gained from improving one's professional skill level and delivering classes more effectively. An empowered, skilled profession is also in a better position to negotiate working terms and conditions

Further reading

'How people learn: Brain, mind, experience and school' by John Bransford and colleagues (2000, National Academies Press) is both a great summary of learning in general, and an excellent example of how research can and has been used to analyse the learning process. It's very balanced, discussing cognitive psychology but also taking into account constructivist perspectives, too.

Discussion questions

- To what extent can a classroom or school be like a laboratory, regularly testing and experimenting in order to find the most effective practices?

- What would it look like if teaching was informed by *neither* experience nor research? (You might want to consider one of the many celebrities, journalists or politicians who have publicly aired their views on how schools could be improved!)

- What promotion pathways might encourage teachers to engage with research? Consider alternative options besides traditional management roles.

Notes

1 See the Donaldson report, Donaldson (2010), available at https://www2.gov.scot/resource/doc/337626/0110852.pdf.
2 Bjork, E.L. and Bjork, R.A. (2011). Making things hard on yourself, but in a good way: Creating desirable difficulties to enhance learning. In Gernsbacher, M.A., Pew, R.W., Hough, L.M., & Pomeranz, J.R. (Eds). *Psychology and the real world: Essays illustrating fundamental contributions to society* (pp. 56–64). New York: Worth Publishers.
3 Sachs, J. (2016). Teacher professionalism: why are we still talking about it? *Teachers and Teaching*, 22(4), 413–425.
4 Firth, J. (2017). Experts in learning. In L. Rycroft-Smith & J. L. Dutaut (Eds.) *Flip the system UK: A teachers' manifesto*. Abingdon, UK: Routledge.
5 Ellis, S. and Smith, V. (2017). Assessment, teacher education and the emergence of professional expertise. *Literacy*, 51(2), 84–93.

Finding time for research

Having considered the purpose of research engagement, it's important to now tackle the thorny issue of finding time for research, especially when it is not officially a part of your role.

When you have a full-to-bursting timetable and a stack of home-work to deal with every night, it is very tempting to say that there is no time for research at all. Perhaps you, or other teachers that you know, feel slightly guilty about this—you know this is something that you are encouraged or even expected to do, but there just isn't time in the day.

This chapter will explore ways of fitting research into your general schedule, and making it part of your daily activities. From the point of view of wellbeing as well as common sense, most teachers can't add a large research burden to an already busy day job. We know (despite the stereotype that teachers have short days and long holidays) that most of us have a very heavy workload—one of the highest number of hours worked of any profession.[1] And there are few other jobs where it is the norm to give multiple presentations every day.

However, as well as talking about fitting research in, this chapter will discuss how research can actually make these issues a little easier. Is the endless marking actually having an impact on learning? Are there simpler ways of structuring classes and materials that would reduce preparation time? Could learners be doing more of the planning and organisation of learning for themselves? And could we find ways to ensure that new learning is retained better, reducing the frenetic pace of most classes?

Pressures on time

At a time when the media are quite rightly highlighting the pressures that teachers face and raising concerns about the thousands who have left the profession, the idea we should engage with the research as well as completing our teaching duties may seem challenging—even unrealistic. Undoubtedly, some (probably most) teachers are already working more than their contracted hours. For many, teaching is already a 6-day-per-week job due to the demands of marking and preparation. Indeed, the round-the-clock expectations—to respond to email, to manage 24/7 virtual learning environments, as well as the associated mental workload—can make the job seem almost non-stop.

This book can't answer problems about workload directly, but research engagement is highly relevant to this issue. For one thing, who better than teachers to research these very issues—do we want to leave it to external researchers to tell us about the pressure we are under, and how to address it? Governments are much more easily persuaded by evidence than by subjective complaints, and teachers can help to set the agenda in terms of finding out the extent, causes and effects of overwork.

Research engagement can also suggest ways of saving time, in particular by cutting out ineffective practices. Numerous myths about learning have been uncovered over the years, and many of these time-wasting strategies—and how to avoid them—are explained later in this book. Some studies and reviews have suggested that homework in the early years is largely ineffective, for example (see From the research on p. 28). This is not necessarily a reason to cut homework out altogether, but perhaps to draw on research when trying to find ways to make homework tasks impactful in a way that does not require excessive teacher preparation and marking/feedback time.

Evidence-informed classroom learning strategies are also more time efficient; Doug Rohrer and Kelli Taylor conducted research into over-learning of maths problems (i.e. continuing to study beyond the point of mastery). In their experiment, they found that studying additional maths problems after pupils had reached a point of mastery (indicated by around 90% correct completion of tasks) made no long-term difference to attainment.[2] Cutting out time-wasting practices leaves more learning time for other tasks and activities which are useful and enjoyable. This can also lead to increases in attainment, which may help to reduce teacher stress.

Where research fits in

Let's think about when and where research fits into your schedule. Compared to many professions, teachers have relatively little flexibility—if you are teaching a class of thirty ten year olds, you have to be present in the classroom most of the time, and therefore can't be in the library or at a research conference! One of the biggest barriers to research engagement is not the lack of time per se, but the lack of flexibility in a teacher's routine.

However, the structured nature of a teacher's week can also be beneficial. Psychologists who look at developing new habits know the benefits of linking new tasks to existing structures. As with exercise or creative writing (budding authors are often encouraged to form an 'hour a day habit'), research engagement is likely to have the greatest impact if it becomes a normal part of your routine. And unlike some workers, teachers often have times that are specifically allocated to professional development and preparation. Areas where time might be carved out within your existing schedule might include:

- Allocating a free period once a week.
- Staying later for half an hour once a week.
- Allocating a period of time every morning after you first arrive, between getting into the school and starting your first lesson.
- The second half of one or more lunch break.

Of course, it may be the case that every spare lunchtime and after school slot is already accounted for, in which case it might be necessary to consider the other part of the equation—what are the other demands on your non-contact time, and could any of these be cut? While such changes may come at a cost, it's a matter of professional judgement to decide whether these other activities, however valuable,

23

are more valuable than ensuring that your teaching practice is evidence informed. What changes you might make depends a lot on your current arrangements, but some possibilities include:

- Dropping regular revision sessions/free ad hoc tutoring.
- For secondary staff, cutting down on feedback on UCAS statements.
- Dropping one or more extracurricular activity.
- Getting out of one or more lunch duty, detention monitoring, or other supervision activities.
- Using in-service days or other professional development time for research engagement instead of whole-school activities.
- Pulling out of time-consuming event organisation.

This is not to suggest that the above functions are unimportant and certainly, for some of them, a degree of negotiation might be necessary with school management. But there is certainly a case to be made that teacher research engagement is every bit as important as other aspects of school life, and that the teacher who is making an effort to engage, enquire and share should be given a lighter burden of responsibility in other areas. You can be sure that some teachers are evading such tasks for less worthy reasons.

In terms of the revision sessions and UCAS help (a feature of many secondary schools), there is a serious argument to be made that extra help is not always so very helpful to pupils in the long run. Scheduled revision sessions are often attended mainly by the more organised and high-achieving pupils who may need it least, and although extra tutoring and guidance may help in the short-term, it is poor preparation for the level of independence required at university.

Changes to practices: preparation

Teachers care about their pupils' progress and work hard to promote learning, and in doing so it is natural therefore to feel that we should always be doing something: standing at the front talking, reviewing written work, helping struggling learners, or engaging in question-and-answer sessions. Most of these tasks have a hidden extra workload in terms of preparation and follow-up.

There is, however, an argument for reducing the amount of information and feedback that we give. Dylan Wiliam argues that feedback on written work should be divided into four parts: a quarter self-marked, a quarter peer marked, a quarter given a 'light touch' feedback from the teacher (for example identifying any major misunderstandings or issues such as length and style), and a quarter with more detailed, line-by-line comments. For many teachers, adopting such an approach could cut their workload considerably—and in doing so, the learners actually improve, as they start to gain more of an independent ability to reflect on their own work and that of others, and figure out improvements for themselves.

As mentioned in the previous chapter, it can be beneficial for feedback to be reduced and delayed, perhaps because this places more onus on the learner to consider and self-evaluate as part of the learning process.[3] Likewise, simply providing information does not always lead to learning (as we have all noticed, from time to time!) Instead a critical element facilitating effective learning is for the learners to effortfully and actively retrieve prior information from mind. As Pooja Agarwal and colleagues have put it, "through the act of retrieval, or calling information to mind, our memory for that information is strengthened and forgetting is less likely to occur".[4]

Technology and classroom organisation approaches can also be used to relieve some of the burden on the teacher. Direct questioning could at times be replaced by paired questions or the use of freely available online quizzes. These kind of changes can free up more of your time for one-to-one support of pupils who are struggling, meaning that lunchtimes or after school times do not need to be used for such activities. And what if the quizzes aren't good enough? Editing or creating a new quiz could be a task assigned to a group of learners; doing so will not only help to consolidate their learning, but also improve their metacognitive awareness of what they are supposed to know.

Case study: blogging homework

The case below is a simple example of how blogs can provide both a useful teaching option and an area of research interest:

Andrei is a Geography teacher. He has been reading a book chapter which talks about applying technology to vary the format of homework, including the use of online quizzes and blogs. He decides that this would be a good area for him to begin engaging with research.

In their topic on biomes in GCSE Geography, Andrei and his colleagues typically set the class an article and questions to tackle every week, with their responses handed in to be marked. However, he knows that in this topic in particular, learners often find the reading dull and hard to grasp, and that they pay little attention to the feedback given. This year, Andrei wants to do things differently.

Andrei is sure that getting pupils to write blog posts would allow a more personalised engagement in the topic, and that learners would listen more to peer feedback. He therefore sets them the task of finding a picture relevant to a biome (e.g. a desert, a rainforest) and using this as the basis of a blog post about whether they would or would not like to visit this place. As a follow-up, all pupils are given time in class to read and comment on each other's posts.

Following this change, Andrei looked for further articles about the use of blogging homework, and subscribed to two blogs on the subject.

As can be seen from Andrei's case, engaging with research doesn't need to be hugely time-consuming. Andrei began by identifying an area of current practice which was unsatisfactory— a set of readings that pupils find dull. In replacing them, he initially referred just to a single book chapter for ideas. However, he then used this as a focus for further ongoing investigation. This narrow focus kept the level of background reading manageable.

He also focused on strategies which reduced workload in terms of marking, thereby offsetting the time spent on research with greater time efficiency in his practice. Better still, the activity is likely to have been memorable for pupils, and led to a meaningful in-class follow-up.

Changes to practice: materials and planning

A further change which is well worth considering is to reduce planning and materials development. Many teachers are starting to question the value of the highly complex and diverse types of lessons that were often encouraged in the past (and still are, in some contexts). A few of the more time-consuming include:

- Making personalised worksheets for different learners.
- Recording or self-assessing your own lessons.
- Photocopying student work and filing it.
- Role-plays, dioramas, or making documentaries.
- Creating games, or anything involving creating multiple sets of cards or laminated instructions.

Some teachers instead find a simple lesson structure that works, and just keep using it—a guilt-free and evidence-based approach that helps keep learners on board (as they enjoy knowing what is expected) and avoids planning or admin time expanding out of control. It certainly needn't mean that lessons are boring or uniform, but that the humour and variety of a lesson derives from interaction with each other and the lesson content. As Teacher Toolkit author Ross Morrison McGill puts it, "Over-planning generally leads to 'under-learning'. Be wary of including too many activities and objectives. Break objectives down, and don't try to cover too much content".[5]

From the research

Key issue: homework can be very time-consuming to mark, but is it effective? It's useful to know—if not, this could be a major area to cut our workload, or at least to transform it in some way. However, the question gives rise to multiple sub-questions: for whom is it effective? When it is currently ineffective, how could we improve it? How can it be made as effective as possible, while minimising the time cost to the teacher?

What the research says: although homework is a near-universal feature of schooling, the evidence supporting its efficacy is unimpressive. Reviews suggest that it has little or no impact on attainment during the primary years, and a modest effect on attainment for middle or high school.[6] Furthermore any benefit for this age group has to be counted against potential costs—beyond a certain point, the cost in terms of learner fatigue start to outweigh the benefit.

Some might argue that even where it has no impact on attainment, homework instils habits of self-discipline that are useful for pupils' later life or study. However, this has also not been clearly evidenced, and it is just as possible for homework to have emotional or motivational costs. Poorly-designed tasks could harm confidence and undermine a learner's natural curiosity. There may also be costs that don't show up in learners' results—missed opportunities to spend time with friends and family, to read, to play games, and so forth.

'Talking homework' (where pupils explain a topic to a family member) and the use of online/app-based quizzes are two options that can be easily implemented, involve little or no preparation time for the teacher, and have a sound evidence base—quick tasks which involve retrieval from memory can boost learning (see Chapter 3) and can also reduce learner anxiety.[7] Using these approaches could reduce stress, increase effectiveness, and can even be integrated into family interactions, games, or other activities.

Where longer, project-type tasks are set, it would make sense to do these as a review, rather than (as is common practice) midway through a topic. For example, if a primary class has studied the Roman civilisation as a topic, the best time to do a solo project on this could be a couple of months later—after mastery of the key content has been achieved, to allow consolidation and tackle forgetting (or, indeed, as a way of integrating learning from more than one topic). Independent learning is challenging especially for young learners, and projects often lack structure; setting clear and short weekly sub-task helps break the work into small steps, avoiding the temptation for parents to take charge.

Focusing your interests

In the previous chapter (Chapter 1), we considered how a broad understanding of research underpins teacher professionalism. However, when thinking about time and workload, it's clear that we also need to find ways of narrowing the scope, and focusing in on particular classroom problems that are relevant to you.

That might seem to be something of a contradiction, and certainly a balance is necessary. Returning to the GP analogy, a general practitioner doctor may choose to specialise on a particular issue (e.g. skin disorders) but cannot ignore the need to stay more broadly informed, in order to tackle the multiple medical issues they encounter every day.

A starting point to reduce the load is to focus on those areas of research that most directly pertain to classroom processes, so that research findings can have a direct impact on how you teach. Some of the most obvious are the following:

- Motivation: how to make learners want to learn, and enthuse them about their topics and projects.
- Memory: how learners understand and remember information over the long term.

- Thinking and mental processing ('cognition'), including processes that are specific to reading and other skills.

- Emotion and behaviour: how learners feel about themselves, their work and other people, their relationships, and how they act in a learning context.

- Understanding and supporting learners with special educational needs, or those from vulnerable backgrounds.

- Understanding how best to make use of technological changes and ICT in an effective, impactful way.

Some other areas—such as the curriculum, educational policy and the history or philosophy of education—are critically important to education in general, but rather harder for the teacher to apply on a day to day basis. You may have no control over what's in the curriculum, for example. Nevertheless, you could choose to make such areas the focus of your personal scholarship. The views and input of practising teachers would greatly add to these research fields, and exciting opportunities could come your way as a result (see also Chapter 14, which focuses on developing a research profile in your subject discipline rather than one that links to pedagogy).

A speciality

The argument above could be taken still further by finding a specific area based on one of the ideas, which you can investigate in detail. This will allow you to really dig into the research, to find and read up-to-date papers with a level of depth that would be too time-consuming if applied to education more generally. What's more, practice in research engagement (as in all things) improves your ability, and you will therefore find that the research becomes quicker to read once you have developed your knowledge in this area.

Which area should you specialise in? It may be that certain things particularly catch your attention from your broader reading. Most teachers have urgent questions about how to improve particular aspects of their practice, perhaps something that has been bothering them, or which they have had negative feedback on. How can I make my learners better remember chemistry definitions? How can I make my instructions clearer? How can I get them into the habit of doing homework accurately and punctually? How can I improve my questioning? Such questions are highly context-specific, but we all have our individual teaching concerns.

Other barriers to teacher engagement

Expertise

Author and educational researcher John Hattie has argued that teachers shouldn't carry out or collaborate on research, saying: "the whole research side, leave that to the academics".[8] However, on the face of it, teachers as graduates and professional educators (many with postgraduate qualifications) are well qualified to conduct research, and many have already done so by the time they enter the profession. Purely academic researchers play an important role, but teacher-researchers and other voices from the profession can make a valuable contribution too.

Lack of journal access

Another obstacle is a lack of the comprehensive library facilities which are standard in most Higher Education (HE) settings—most teachers have limited access to research journals (if any). However, access to resources is easier than in the past due to increased open access and the sharing of resources on the internet. Numerous journals make at least some content freely available, and many researchers make pre-prints (their first submitted draft, rather than the final published version) freely available online. The Chartered College of Teaching have a research database available to their members, and in Scotland, there is the General Teaching Council for Scotland (GTCS)'s useful EBSCO research collection. In addition, many researchers or labs list their publications online with links to pdf copies of the articles (and if they do not, it can be worth emailing a researcher directly to ask for a copy).

Practical location

Teachers are often not in the same physical location as those with whom they might like to collaborate, and it is hard to access conferences (especially for full-time classroom staff). However, some barriers are mitigated slightly compared to previous years due to the ease of networking and sharing resources online. The need for face-to-face meetings is reduced by the use of technology such as Google Hangouts, and many conferences and Continuing Professional Development (CPD) events feature live streaming of talks.

Funding

A lot of research is funded externally, and/or is part of a researcher's salaried role (and therefore, in effect, funded). Time and money are at a premium in the education system, with widespread cuts to support staff; it's unlikely that schools are going to pay you to make research part of your role, release you from classroom duties, or fund you to run research projects. However, it should be noted that anyone can apply for funding; it's not impossible for school staff to do so (some opportunities are only available to those with a doctorate, but this just means that those who do not have one need someone else to act as a principal investigator). In future, it would be great to see the establishment of more funding specifically for teacher-research. In the meantime, why not ask whichever organisation you work for (local authority, multi-academy trust, etc) to allocate small-scale research funding that teachers could bid for, in order to fund classroom cover, travel and admin costs. If they are asking you to add research to your workload, it's the least they can do!

Publication

While it may seem that publication of your research is an impossibly high hurdle, there is another way to look at this issue. Academics don't find publication easy, either, and they are under considerably more pressure to do it—their jobs literally depend on it. Teachers can be quite flexible about how and when they share their research outputs, with no particular need to aim for peer-reviewed journals or to write lengthy articles (5000 words or more is standard for a journal article, while a piece in a teaching magazine might be a fraction of this). Chartered College's 'Impact' is a peer-reviewed journal which publishes research by school teachers, though more outlets are needed (see Chapter 17 for more suggestions on this issue).

Research project: given the importance of finding time for engaging with research, time management could be an interesting focus for an investigation of your own working practices, and this could also pave the way for a later study of other staff.

How to do it: this study will involve measuring how you are using your time, and exploring different methods for gathering data on this issue.

As you might expect, people are not always accurate when trying to remember how long something took, or exactly what they have been doing. For this reason, it would be interesting to explore at least two options for recording your own working habits.

First select a regular hour or two in your weekly schedule which you spend working on planning, marking, materials development, and suchlike. Next, pick a way of recording data about your time use during this session. Options include:

- You can set a phone alarm or notification to go off periodically, for example every 20 minutes. When it does, take a note of what you were working on immediately prior to this.

(continued)

(continued)

- A written reflection at the end of the session, where you describe from memory what you achieved.

- Making a before-and-after comparison of the tasks themselves, and record some numerical data such as how many assignments you marked, or how many words you wrote.

- If your work is entirely screen-based, you could use one of the apps which track phone or laptop use.

Try at at least two of these methods, using them on more than one occasion. Now reflect on the data that you gathered, comparing the different methods that you used. Does anything surprise you? Are there notable differences in the usefulness and accuracy of the data between these different methods, or any important omissions?

As noted, this could be developed into a broader study of staff once you have selected a method that you think is reliable; please refer to the chapter on ethics (Chapter 8) before gathering any new data from other people. Chapters 11–12 explore in detail some of the main methods of gathering data.

Concluding comments

There is no doubt that some research activities will take up time, especially if you aim to develop a deep level of knowledge of the issue under investigation and/or choose to share your findings more widely with other teachers. However, many activities can be fitted in as a normal part of professional practice. Indeed, along with the concern that 'we don't have time for this', another frequent comment from teachers on the issue of research engagement is 'we are already doing this, as part of our professional reflection'.

Research activities can be motivating, can provide variety, and bring with them an increased sense of professional confidence—all issues that are known to mitigate stress. Engaging with and in research, then, is not likely to drive teachers from the profession complaining of added workload, but can make them feel refreshed, engaged, and empowered.

Further reading

Ross Morrison McGill's 'Mark. Plan. Teach: Save time, reduce workload, impact learning' (2018, Bloomsbury) is a useful guide to how workload can be, in part, a planning issue. The book helps to explain how a more streamlined process can also be more effective.[9]

'The productive researcher' by Mark Reed (2017, Fast Track Impact) is an excellent book for anyone who worries about how they can find the time for research activities. The author shows researchers how they can become more productive in a fraction of their current working day, drawing on interviews with some of the world's highest performing researchers. Although aimed mainly at university staff, it shows the teacher that just as in schools, some university-based researchers are much more productive than others, and asks the question 'why?'. It is a very practical guide to getting more out of the limited time available to any busy professional.

Discussion questions

- What tasks and pastimes could you potentially stop or reduce in order to make more time, and out of these, which would you be willing to stop?
- It might be possible to reduce workload by cutting out ineffective teaching practices. What aspects of teaching practice do you think require further investigation to see whether they are effective? Is there anything you are currently forced to do that you are sure is a waste of time? And is it possible that engaging in research may actually save you time in the long run?
- Do you consider flipped learning (where learners study new concepts at home and then do homework-style exercises in class) to be a potential time saver? Or could it consume a lot of time, for

example if it involves creating an entirely new set of video-based learning materials?

- How do you plan to balance out the need to develop a broad-based understanding of education with the advantages of specialising in a particular area?

Notes

1 Wiggins, K (2015, 27 Feb). Teachers work more overtime than any other professionals, analysis finds. *TES*. Accessed 02 February 2016 at https://www.tes.com/news/school-news/breaking-news/teachers-work-more-overtime-any-other-professionals-analysis-finds
2 Taylor, K., & Rohrer, D. (2010). The effects of interleaved practice. *Applied Cognitive Psychology*, 24(6), 837–848.
3 Yan, V. X., Clark, C. M., & Bjork, R. A. (2016). Memory and metamemory considerations in the instruction of human beings revisited: Implications for optimizing online learning. In J. C. Horvath, J. Lodge, & J. A. C. Hattie (Eds) *From the laboratory to the classroom: Translating the learning sciences for teachers* (pp. 61–78). Abingdon, UK: Routledge.
4 Agarwal, P. K., Roediger, H. L., McDaniel, M. A., & McDermott, K. B. (2018). How to use retrieval practice to improve learning. *Retrieval Practice*. Retrieved 14 October 2018 from http://pdf.retrievalpractice.org/RetrievalPracticeGuide.pdf (page 2).
5 McGill, R. (2018). Lesson planning. *The Profession: The Annual Publication for Early Career Teachers*. Retrieved 26 November 2018 from https://impact.chartered.college/article/mcgill-lesson-planning/
6 EEF (2018). Teaching and learning toolkit (October 2018). *Education Endowment Foundation Website*. Retrieved 26 January 2019 from https://educationendowmentfoundation.org.uk/public/files/Toolkit/complete/EEF-Teaching-Learning-Toolkit-October-2018.pdf
7 Agarwal, P. K., D'Antonio, L., Roediger III, H. L., McDermott, K. B., & McDaniel, M. A. (2014). Classroom-based programs of retrieval practice reduce middle school and high school students' test anxiety. *Journal of Applied Research in Memory and Cognition*, 3(3), 131–139.
8 Stewart, W. (2015, 22 April). Leave research to the academics, John Hattie tells teachers. *TES*. Retrieved 13 October 2018 from https://www.tes.com/news/leave-research-academics-john-hattie-tells-teachers
9 McGill, R (2017) *Mark. Plan. Teach: Save time, reduce workload, impact learning*. London: Bloomsbury Education.

Accessing and using research evidence

As discussed in the previous chapters, published evidence from research studies should not replace our experience or professional judgement, but supplement and enhance it. However, it is one thing for a teacher to have a desire to be evidence-informed in their teaching practice, and quite another to find the right information from among the mass of research studies out there. Here we will consider the many sources of research findings, the types of sources you may need to use, and how to interpret and understand what you read.

Narrowing the scope of reading

Now that you have (formally or informally) considered an area of research that you would like to focus on (see Chapter 2), it's time to delve into the literature on that topic. You will no doubt want to gain familiarity with what is currently happening in this specific field—the cutting-edge research. However, it's also useful to put this into context by broadening your awareness of historical issues. What are the classic findings in this particular area, and what big questions have occupied the field? Try looking up the index of one or more general textbooks on education or psychology, or speaking to someone who already has some expertise in the area.

Other options to consider as a starting point for your background reading are:

- A popular book: whether written by teachers or by academic researchers who want to reach professionals and the general public, popular books that aim to make a topic accessible can be an excellent way of developing a broad understanding of a topic before delving into specific research studies. A good example is Carol Dweck's 'Mindset' (2006), which summarises and popularises the conclusions from earlier academic work done by her lab.

- A chapter: as above, except shorter—an author may have contributed a chapter to a longer work. Such chapters can succinctly summarise the key issues relating to your topic. Sean Kang's chapter on interleaving in 'From the laboratory to the classroom' (see further reading on p. 52) does this very well.

- News articles and blogs: although it won't cover an issue in the same kind of depth, a news story or blog post may stimulate your thinking on an issue that you were previously unaware of, and give you a starting point by citing particular concepts or researchers that you can then look up and find out more about.

Also, bear in mind that anyone on the internet can start a blog, and the most evangelical supporters of an idea often do. Such writers can tend to over-state the evidence, and their writing often contains a heavy side-serving of opinion. Such blogs can provide ideas, references and examples from practice, but they can also mislead you by presenting one-sided or out-of-date findings as if they are incontrovertible facts. While news articles from some sources may be more reliable, in most cases there is very little difference nowadays. Indeed, education blog posts are often better researched and more detailed than news articles, and have the advantage that they tend to be written by teachers rather than journalists.

It's important to recognise that some books and chapters will be significantly out of date, biased or otherwise flawed. Any published source is going to be limited in terms of recent developments that it mentions. However, such sources are an excellent starting point, especially when combined with an internet search for recent articles.

Sources of research evidence

Engaging with research involves an element of coming to recognise academic conventions, and learning what kind of sources publish useful work. Some of the key sources of evidence that could help to inform your practice are as follows:

Original research articles

A research journal is a periodical publication aimed at academics and other experts in a field, and which publishes work on a specific topic. An original research article in such a journal presents a novel piece of scholarship, often (though not always) with a new set of data. Such articles are usually *peer-reviewed,* meaning that two or more experts in the field have anonymously read and commented on the article prior to publication; peer reviewers can reject weak or flawed articles, so this is often taken as a mark of quality.

However, there are a vast number of journals of varying standing, some of which publish work in exchange for a fee. Once you have identified your main areas of research interest, have a look at what journals the most prominent researchers publish in (this is easy to find—most researchers list their publications on a personal or university web page). You can also look at a journal's impact factor—a number based on how often recent articles from that journal get cited. Higher is better; anything above 1 is good, above 5 indicates a very prominent journal, and the top worldwide titles can exceed 20 (*Nature* has an impact factor of around 30). The numbers are based on how many other researchers cite work from the journal.[1]

It's a good sign (in terms of transparency) if the journal's website displays its impact factor and policies. It should also list its editorial board. The names of these people may not be familiar to you, but they are a good indication of the kind of research a journal will publish, and its quality. A few minutes spent Googling the names of the editorial board to find out where they work and what their academic experience is will tell you a lot about a journal.

Review articles

Exciting and noteworthy though a new finding may be, the results from a single study are not enough for us to draw firm conclusions. Instead, the research needs to be *replicated*. Replication means repeating the study with exactly the same methodology, in order to compare the new results with the original set of findings.

Over time, a finding might be replicated multiple times, at which point it starts to be accepted as fact by the scientific community. Some journal articles collate such findings, and present an overview. These are known as review studies or review articles, and they help to overcome any bias inherent in the work of a particular researcher or team. There are various types; one of the most important is the 'systematic review', which tries to take on board all research that meets a set of criteria, for example all experiments on a particular topic published within a certain range of dates. While not immune to bias, systematic reviews are transparent in their methods (and can themselves be replicated).

Simplified research

It's not always necessary to tackle original journal articles, especially in the early stages of your research engagement when you are aiming to get a broad and quick overview of the main issues. Many books present simplified summaries, including (less commonly) summaries of a single research article, or (more commonly) syntheses of the research on a particular area. These are excellent gateways into the research, ahead of tackling more lengthy original work (see further reading, below, for recommendations). However, as with textbooks, they may suffer from a degree of oversimplification.

Prepared summaries and syntheses

Finally, a key source of research evidence for many schools and educational authorities are the secondary sources produced by teaching bodies and other institutions, and presented as easily and quickly digested overviews.

A good example of this is the 'Teaching and Learning Toolkit' made by the Educational Endowment Foundation (EEF), often referred to as the EEF toolkit. This covers a broad range of strategies from collaborative learning to the role of homework, each categorised in terms of their cost and how secure (according to EEF's review) the evidence is. A strength of this toolkit is that it provides references to the original sources on which the conclusions are based, most of which are systematic reviews and meta-analyses.

However, a limitation of this type of digest is that it takes little account of the quality of its sources. For example, the EEF gives learning styles a rating of 2/5 for the security of the evidence, despite acknowledging in the same document that learning styles do not exist (see Chapter 4), and that any gains observed must be due to other variables. This perhaps highlights the dangers of accepting simplistic ideas about 'what works' without understanding the underlying theories and psychological processes.[2]

How to read and critique a journal article

As teachers, we don't want our pupils to accept things uncritically. Instead, we want them to make judgements of quality and purpose: to recognise that some books and poems are better than others, and to be aware of the potential bias in sources that they read. We want creative arts and sports learners to recognise the importance of context and communication, while science and social science pupils need to be aware of competing explanations for findings rather than accepting everything they are taught as fact, particularly as they progress to the later years of school and start to realise that many traditional scientific theories are incomplete or flawed.

In a similar way, the teacher who seeks to use research well and to the benefit of their classes needs to recognise the biases and agendas that characterise a lot of educational research. This doesn't mean that the research literature is dishonest, but simply that it has a real-world context and that it is written by human beings with varied experiences, aims and values. Sometimes two popular theories have implications which are inconsistent with each other—they can't both be right. And of course, even very good researchers are sometimes plain wrong in their conclusions.

The task of the reader

The challenges of reading a research source are much like those presented by any form of reading. Researchers know that people who claim to be speed readers (as opposed to just very fast readers—those at the faster end of the normal range), are typically using a set of techniques, the most critical of which is inference. Rather than reading every word, such readers skim the text, and then use their real-world knowledge to fill in any gaps.

In fact, all readers do this to an extent, and we make more use of it the more experienced we become as readers. However, literacy researchers now recognise that reading skill is highly context-dependent.[3] Even as a teacher, a graduate and an expert in your own subject, you may find some forms of technical writing difficult to make sense of, while the writers of such texts find them straightforward, and may struggle with your subject area. How easily could you read the technical manual for a computer component or a discussion of the political landscape in the late Mayan empire? These differences reveal that reading ability is not a matter of intelligence. Instead, there are two key aspects that affect the difficulty of the text:

- The reader's relevant background knowledge. It is difficult to make sense of a text if you know little or nothing about the subject matter. Hirsch uses the example of sports; can you make sense of a sentence such as "Jones sacrificed and knocked in a run." What about "The leg spinner—previously a white-ball specialist—played in all five tests, but was used sparingly in a series dominated by seam"..?[4] What such sporting examples (baseball and cricket, respectively) demonstrate is how much a reader brings to a text, and that without the background knowledge in a particular domain, it's very hard to make sense of what we read.

- The conventions of the form. Language conventions are most obvious in forms such as poetry and drama writing, but every type of writing has its own conventions. Scientific and social science writing has its own vocabulary and assumptions, which can make it somewhat impenetrable to the uninitiated.

If you are new to reading education research, it's likely that you will struggle with both of the above areas to some extent. Key terms and cited authors will be unfamiliar to you, and the articles may be talking about issues or education systems that you know little about and using methodology that you have never directly experienced. Likewise, you may lack a familiarity with the unspoken rules of the genre, although this will depend on your own academic background—social science teachers may find them relatively accessible, while those with a biology or neuroscience background will find the format of cognitive science papers fairly easy to follow.

While your background and knowledge and awareness of conventions are still developing, it's unlikely that you will be able to read journal articles rapidly, skimming them as you might do with a newspaper article.

From the research

Key issue: does re-reading leads to better learning? Repeatedly reading notes or textbook chapters is a popular strategy among school pupils, and widely recommended by teachers, too.[5] What issues does this have, and what other alternatives might we recommend?

What the research says: for both pupils and teachers alike, reading alone suffers from being an overly passive way of learning. Multiple re-readings of a text appears to be an ineffective way to learn its content. It tends to lead to fairly rapid forgetting, with an immediate sense of familiarity but loss of the key details within a few days. What's more, reading the text more than once seems

(continued)

(continued)

to have very little impact in terms of memory for details (though it could be more useful in situations where a second reading is necessary to fully understand a text). A delayed return to the text is likely to be more valuable.

Research indicates that learners also have a very poor judgement of how well they know something after they have initially read about or heard it—perhaps helping to explain why re-reading remains such a popular study strategy. If asked to predict how they will do in a future test, these predictions tend not to match their eventual grade! In other words, it typically leads to poor *metacognitive judgement* of learning.

However, if learners' judgements are delayed, or if they are given a quick quiz or other demanding task before making a judgement of learning, their estimates are more accurate.[6]

Retrieval practice—actively retrieving the information from memory to help to consolidate memory and understanding—is a principle that can apply to your own professional learning. If you test yourself in some way or otherwise retrieve information (writing notes from memory, discussing it, etc) then you are less likely to forget what you have studied, and you may have a better awareness of how well you know it, too. Therefore in your professional reading, aim to summarise research that you read in a closed-book format, at least a day after first reading it. A similar benefit could be gained by blogging about the research, or forming a teaching and learning discussion group which reads and discusses a new article at each meeting. Either way, you have to actively retrieve the information from mind. Of course, it's all right to check the original or your notes, too!

The format of a research paper

Although it is difficult to make generalisations about research articles because they do vary widely by topic and depending on where they were published, there are common features in terms of structure and format of empirical papers (i.e. those that present new data) which you will see again and again:

- An abstract. This is a short summary of the whole piece. Its purpose is to allow readers to gauge whether the paper is relevant to them, and is therefore worth reading in full.

- An introduction/literature review. This is where the researcher presents the rationale for the paper by reviewing previous studies and identifying a gap in knowledge. Usually they refer to one or more theories, and from these make a prediction (the 'hypothesis') about what they are going to find.

- Methodology. Often subdivided into different sections, this presents factual details about how the study was done. Here you can find out who the participants were, what the task was, how long it took, etc. Frequently, however, this section is kept quite brief, and you may have to refer to supporting material online and/or contact the researcher to find out some details.

- Results. Here the researcher presents the findings in a fairly objective way, using tables and graphs to highlight key points.

- Discussion, the final main section. This is where the researcher reflects on the findings, links them back to the theories described earlier, and comes to a conclusion.

In longer papers, short versions of these sections may be repeated multiple times as different studies are described, followed by a longer 'general discussion' which ties the whole argument together. Naturally, most papers also include references, which are either shown as footnotes or as a reference list at the end—a choice which mainly depends on the journal/publisher.

Picking the articles

One rule of thumb that is especially helpful for people who are new to tackling educational research is not to overcomplicate things, or bite off more than you can chew. Consider the following guidelines when choosing articles to read:

> *Choose an area where you are already familiar with the scientific conventions, and have some relevant background knowledge.*

Why dive into sociological theory if you are a biology teacher? There are dozens of relevant papers on educational neuroscience which would be an easier starting point.

> *Pick something short and accessibly written.*

It might sound simplistic, but as with any area of education, it makes sense to start with an easy-to-read text, and build up. Nobody gives Shakespeare to a 5 year old, and for good reason! Tackling something very difficult is likely to be off-putting and you won't learn much from a paper that you don't finish or don't understand.

Think of reading articles as a process, with a certain amount of output in a given time. How many pages can you read in ten minutes, allowing for fatigue and breaks? Allocate yourself some reading time, and then do the necessary arithmetic. For example, if you have a 30-minute train journey home, how many pages will you read at your typical reading speed? Could you manage it in one, or at least two journeys?

> *Don't be afraid to stop.*

Finally, if an article, after being initially promising, turns out to be irrelevant, turgidly written or just plain boring, give up and move onto something else. Some researchers are much better writers than others! And what is boredom, anyway . . . ? Often it stems at least partly from irrelevance of the content or the reader's failure to understand (or both), and could therefore suggest that this particular article isn't telling you anything that will be of use.

If giving up seems too negative, by all means file it in a 'to read' folder for the future. Perhaps in a year or so, having already established a broader grounding in the research area, you will return to the piece and find it much easier to digest.

One caveat with this recommendation: don't be put off by an article with a message which doesn't fit what you believe and expect. Such contrary findings are often the most useful. They may show aspects of your current thinking that needs to be reappraised. Even if you are not persuaded by the writers of such papers, it can be useful to have a summary which presents a contrary view (and see below on writing a critique). Often papers which disagree with the mainstream view are widely cited, as they present ideas that generate discussion, and can become the go-to counterargument in any summary/review (see also the discussion of 'confirmation bias' in the next chapter).

Case study: the collector

How much research should we attempt to absorb before we choose to act on it? On the one hand, making educational decisions before fully reviewing the background evidence may lead to flawed actions. Essentially, this is the argument in favour of becoming a research-engaged teacher which is made throughout this book! However, there is also the risk—sometimes nicknamed 'analysis paralysis'—of spending too much time looking at the evidence, while putting off the decisions until later. Consider the following case:

> Lauren is a primary teacher, and plays the role of school lead on dyslexia and pupil support. She is hugely interested in the psychology of reading, and has been blogging on this topic for more than a year. She regularly receives email bulletins from journal publishers, and pastes the abstracts of relevant new articles into a document. Every so often, she writes a summary of a particular issue, and adds this to a folder on her computer, and to a file at work.
>
> Recently it has been a particularly busy time, and with such a heavy workload, Lauren has not found as much time

(continued)

47

(continued)

to read the research, and no time at all to digest it. She has, however, been saving the email bulletins without taking any further action.

Lauren's level of research engagement is impressive. However, it is worth questioning to what end she is amassing such an encyclopaedic list of research in her area of interest. It's arguably better to have a working familiarity with a few dozen articles that have a genuine relevance to your needs than to attempt to keep track of hundreds without really using them or remembering the details. Likewise, when tackling new research, it could be more valuable over the long run for her to focus on a smaller number of articles and ensure that she is really taking the time to understand them.

Some aspects of Lauren's research engagement is rather passive—pasting abstracts into a document. This will be time-consuming, and it's hard to see what it would actually lead to. It could be better for her to summarise each paper, forming an annotated bibliography which could grow over time (best of all if initially done from memory, and after a delay). Her blog posts could be a great way of summarising the research from memory, and she could then check back to the details of the original studies when editing each post.

Saving lots of articles without taking any action is like an ever expanding to-do list. The chances are that she'll never come back to most of them. It will be useful for her to save some items, but only if this is sustainable, and she is reading them fairly soon.

Developing your critical awareness

You may hear such overwhelming positivity about certain fashionable educational theories and ideas that you feel there is little need to look for the flaws. Quite simply, it can appear as if everyone agrees and there is no real need for a debate on a matter! However, for the sake of our pupils as well as our own professionalism, it's best to be suspicious about such a cosy consensus. As is widely recognised in politics, people with similar views tend to gravitate together. This can mean that within your own circle of friends or social media bubble, you simply aren't being exposed to any naysayers.

Likewise, as discussed in the previous chapters, certain highly popular ideas in education may simply be fads: fashionable but flimsy ideas that make little difference to learning and are soon dropped from the educational agenda. We don't often hear about things like multiple intelligences, Brain Gym, or left- and right-brained learners these days. Many of the ideas that have fallen by the wayside were based on inadequate evidence, were the work of a very small number of researchers who managed to get a national or global platform, or (if there was a sound research basis) were distorted in the process of being applied to the classroom (for more on educational fads and myths, see Chapter 4).

Could some of today's ideas be subject to the same slide out of fashion? At least some of today's trends (including retrieval practice; see From the research on p. 43) are based on a more comprehensive research foundation, but it's still important for the research-informed teacher to be critical. After all, the advocates of these ideas don't always tell you the limitations!

One of the simplest ways of bootstrapping a critique, if you haven't come across one and the flaws of an idea or study don't immediately occur to you, is simply to ask what the other side of the story is. And you can find this out—easily. Here are several ways of doing it:

- Use the 'cited by' tool on Google Scholar to find other research studies that have mentioned the study. The chances are that some will present a negative side.

- Email or speak to one or more current researcher in the field, or attend a conference (or watch one online).

- Start a discussion about the theory or research paper on a social media site such as Twitter, using an appropriate hashtag.

- Keep asking, 'what is the evidence for this?' (I ask this so often that my children have started doing it; it makes them rather cynical at times, but also less likely to fall for fads!).

- Don't accept any argument on the lines of, 'experts say . . .' or 'this is known to work . . .'. What experts? What evidence is there that it works? How can you be sure that there aren't a dozen other studies that say the opposite?

- As a last resort, Google for '*Flaws with* . . . (insert theory or research field)', or a similar search term! This won't give you all the answers, but may at least give you some leads to work with. Even Wikipedia pages usually include a section on the limitations of theories.

How much is enough?

A common question asked by education students is how much background they need for a particular essay or research project. It's a difficult one to answer. There is no point at which scholarship stops, at which you have done enough. However, you can undoubtedly reach a point—particularly within a niche area—where you have read most of the really seminal works (at least, the recent ones), such that you can provide a background that doesn't have any major gaps in it, even if it is not entirely comprehensive.

Research project: any research project benefits from a careful reading of relevant past findings. Practice these skills by carrying out some focused reading on a particular topic, and establish a list of ten or twelve key sources.

How to do it: begin by looking at a general textbook source (such as a textbook chapter about long-term memory). This will give you a good essential grounding in the general underlying concepts.

As you read, take a note of any terminology that is unfamiliar, writing a one-sentence definition.

Next, find a scholarly chapter from an edited volume on a specific aspect (for example, a chapter about retrieval practice). As you read through it, take a note of the researchers' names which are frequently mentioned, or any cited articles which sound especially important, such as ones that are referred to several times or are described as classics.

Finally, use a search engine such as Google Scholar (or a research database, if you have access to one) to find the articles that you have listed, reading them in full or saving them for later. Also, carry out a search using the list of researcher names that you have made and filtering by year, in order to find out what the major researchers in your chosen area have been working on. Perhaps you could follow this up by checking their academic websites, or even following them on Twitter or LinkedIn.

In this way, you can establish a list of perhaps twenty or so articles or chapters, and then begin to cut this down slightly, discarding ones that seem less relevant. Overall, this process should lead to your having accessed approximately a dozen studies in full—a very good starting level of research background for your own practical study, or simply to be fully aware of the key issues before applying the concept in the classroom.

Concluding comments

This chapter has discussed how it is much easier to take in new information if you already have a comprehensive foundation of basic knowledge in the form of theories, definitions and key concepts. This is just as true for the teacher engaging with research as it is for their learners.

We have also looked at different sources of research. In general, these present a continuum from the more easily digested but possibly flawed and biased summaries, to the more accurate but also more complex original sources and reviews.

Further reading

'How to use retrieval practice to improve learning' by researchers Pooja Agarwal, Henry Roediger, Mark McDaniel and Kathleen McDermott (2018) is an excellent free guide, available from the retrievalpractice.org website.[7]

'From the laboratory to the classroom', edited by Jared Horvath, Jason Lodge and John Hattie (2016, Routledge), is a great example of an edited volume with chapters by experts in their field, each of which succinctly sums up a topic relating to education.

Maryanne Wolf's 'Proust and the squid' (2008, Icon Books) is a really accessible summary of the science of reading.

Discussion questions

- Is it better to focus on reading books or journal articles?
- What are your favourite educational books? Do you feel that you have gained a broad background, or are there areas where you would benefit from further reading on the basic theories?
- What articles would you recommend to colleagues? And what features, do you think, make these especially relevant and useful?
- What reading habits would you encourage a fellow teacher-researcher to engage in? For example, are there particular times of day when you read, or approaches that help you get the most from your reading?

Notes

1 Some minor local journals are not eligible for an impact factor rating, but you can still get a general idea of their quality by looking at their website, checking the editorial board and scanning through recent articles.
2 For this exact reason, author Marc Smith and I wrote 'Psychology in the Classroom' (2018, Routledge) with the aims of both explaining evidence-based strategies and making the underlying psychological theories accessible.

3 Shanahan, T., and Shanahan, C. (2008). Teaching disciplinary literacy to adolescents: Rethinking content-area literacy. *Harvard Educational Review*, 78(1), 40–59.

4 Source: https://www.theguardian.com/sport/2018/sep/28/adil-rashid-england-test-central-contract

5 Morehead, K., Rhodes, M. G., and DeLozier, S. (2016). Instructor and student knowledge of study strategies. *Memory*, 24(2), 257–271.

6 Bui, Y., Pyc, M. A., and Bailey, H. (2018). When people's judgments of learning (JOLs) are extremely accurate at predicting subsequent recall: the "Displaced-JOL effect". *Memory*, 26(6), 771–783.

7 https://www.retrievalpractice.org/library

Will this work for my learners?

The previous chapter focused on finding and critiquing research studies and theories. Such ideas relate to the question of 'what works' in education, and it's important to analyse this issue in a thorough and unbiased way.

However, how can you be sure that what is thought to work (in general) will work for you, your subject and your learners? Perhaps the research you have found on motivation, memory or identity was largely conducted on university students. It might be methodologically sound, but does it actually apply to your setting? Likewise, it's important to be sure that guidance on any area is applicable to the particular learner or group of learners sitting in front of you.

This chapter guides you through the process of generalising research principles from the research literature to your own context.

What is generalising?

Any attempt to justify an educational decision on the basis that 'research says x' faces a fundamental problem: past research can only tell us what happened at a particular time, in a particular setting. Even if a great many studies have found similar things (that a behaviour intervention appears to be beneficial, for example), there is no simple guarantee that it will work well with your pupils.

To put this issue into scientific terms, a researcher selects a **sample**—a smaller group to study, which is assumed to be similar to the greater whole (you can think of other examples of this word like soil samples or urine samples—the principle is the same!). They then attempt to **generalise** the findings of research from the sample (the people who were studied) to a broader group—all primary school learners, say. This broader group is known as the target population. The researcher (or someone else who reads the research) may then decide to apply any implications to a new context:

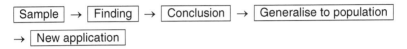

Generalising involves drawing conclusions from the findings of one or more studies conducted on samples of participants, and then relating these findings to the broader population.

Any educational research is necessarily tied to a particular sample, time and context. This doesn't mean the studies in question are flawed, but it's hard to say with certainty that such findings would be repeated even in a study with identical methodology (a 'replication'), never mind when applied in an entirely new way.

Factors affecting generalisations

Making a sound generalisation depends on various factors. One is how **representative** the research's sample are compared to the broader group of learners. If the sample had characteristics that made them unusual in some way, then it may not be possible to say that a conclusion from the research can be generalised to other people.

Let's briefly think about what makes a sample representative. Imagine that you are a primary teacher, interested in what helps children to learn to read, and choose to study your own class. In the course of this research, you might find that certain techniques seem to help, and write a report about them. However, your sample may not actually be similar to the target population (all new readers).[1]

As another example, if a study found that a group of pupils who were at an after-school study group benefited from using a particular mnemonic when revising, you may question whether the sample in this study were sufficiently representative. Perhaps they were unusually high in ability or motivation, and the same strategy might be useless or even counterproductive when used with different subject matter. On the basis of this evidence alone, it would be difficult to be sure.

Similar considerations apply to the specific techniques and materials used in the research, too. If researchers try to engage young readers using a set of reading books about playing cricket, these will be more motivating in areas of the world where cricket is a popular sport.

Typically, of course, we are not generalising from a single study—there may be a large body of research on a particular educational issue. Nevertheless, some of the same issues still apply. Was most of this research done in a particular country/education system? Were the studies as a whole done on different age groups to your classes? Were the participants volunteers, who might therefore have been motivated to make the study work? If the answer to any of these questions is 'yes', it would be best to proceed with caution.

The foregoing shows the importance of depth and quality in the prior research, but it's not easy for a new researcher to gauge this. A review study (see Chapter 2) tries to summarise all of the major research on an issue, and the better ones give more weighting to studies with sound methodology.

Case study: Technique Z

Applying the findings or conclusions from research sources is difficult to do without a degree of bias, especially when your knowledge of the original research is limited. Remember that everyone has an agenda of some kind, and that findings which have been presented as worthwhile and exciting can be overstated, and may disappear if you try to make use of them in your context. Consider the following case:

Rebecca works in a chain of schools. She has established a popular blog about her subject area, Mathematics, and a large Twitter following. Recently she came across a new concept called *Technique Z*—a method which claims to improve attainment in maths by using music and visuals.

Rebecca spent an afternoon reading blog posts about Technique Z, all of which were positive and convincing. As Rebecca is in the middle of completing a Masters in Educational Studies, she decided to focus her dissertation on the use of Technique Z with a class of her own maths pupils.

What is apparent from Rebecca's case is her admirable passion for engaging with research into maths learning, her drive to make her practice evidence-based, and her willingness to share this journey. However, there is a danger that her selection of sources is quite narrow. Education has suffered from a number of notable misconceptions and **neuromyths** (see From the research on p. 61)—supposedly neuroscience-based strategies which have been dismissed by later research. There is a chance that Technique Z is just another fad, not genuinely supported by a more objective look at the evidence.

If Rebecca were to apply Technique Z in her own classroom it could have little or no effect, or even be harmful. New ideas can be exciting, but being research-informed sometimes means being cautious, and selecting ideas with a deeper research base, rather than the technique of greatest current interest.

Bias in research

As the case study on Technique Z shows, it can be easy to fall into the trap of subscribing to a fashionable new idea which appears to be evidence-based. In any area of research, it's important to ask 'what is the evidence?' but also to understand the limitations of what research can tell us. Viewing research findings as a set of instructions for good teaching is over-simplistic.

The existence of bias doesn't necessarily mean that researchers are trying to lie to us, but could relate to flaws in their analysis or methodological choices that affect the results of their study, or even just a slightly skewed perspective in terms of the research questions that they chose to ask.

For example, imagine that a school has brought in a new homework regime which involves pupils being asked to read every night instead of doing written work. Now imagine that researchers make a comparison of Year 11 academic attainment before and after the new initiative was introduced, by comparing last year's test scores with this year's. It's possible that any improvement could be due to the homework, but it's also possible that some other factor could be affecting outcomes. Perhaps, for example, there have been staff changes, or the new cohort of pupils are simply academically stronger than the last one, and would have done better regardless of what type of homework they did (Chapter 8 goes into more detail about how to control such variables and make fair comparisons).

There is also natural human tendency to focus more on ideas that fit our assumptions: **confirmation bias**. This cognitive bias leads to people noticing and remembering things that support their view, and forgetting or ignoring information which goes against it. This bias is known for its role in maintaining prejudices and political assumptions—if you think that public transport is bad, for example, then you may remember examples of buses breaking down and trains being cancelled, while ignoring the large majority of times when they run well and on time.

In research, confirmation bias could be an issue where both the producers and consumers of research focus on and inflate positive results. A closely related issue is the 'file drawer effect', where negative or neutral results are seen as less interesting, and therefore never make it out of the file drawer and onto the pages of a journal article. Cumulatively, this could lead to an educational intervention being seen in a much better light than it deserves!

In your own practice, it's understandable that you may become very interested in a particular theory that you have been reading about and using, but it's also important to recognise that our understanding as educators is still growing, and so is the research field. It might even be best to assume at first that an interesting new idea is a bad one, while remaining open to persuasion. In other words, remain open-minded, but ask a lot of questions, and expect to see sound, well-evidenced explanations of why a new idea could be useful to you, rather than rushing to make changes. Ultimately, a good evidence-based practitioner is a sceptical one.

Other teachers and school leaders are subject to conformation bias, too. All too often, ideas about research are based on hearsay—experienced teachers say that this works, so I had better do it. 'Fads' often do have a smattering of research evidence behind them, but this has been distorted by a combination of bias and enthusiasm (sometimes motivated by financial incentives on the part of people pushing new ideas).

How often do you hear a comment such as, 'They say Technique Z really helps (insert group of children)' . . . ? The first question we can start asking as research-informed practitioners is, 'Can you show me the evidence behind that idea?'. If they can't provide it—or just resort to vague statements such as 'it's obvious' or 'it's well established'—then be very wary of making any changes to your teaching practice. And if the evidence derives from learners very different from your own, you would need to see a clear explanation of why it would generalise.

Principles of generalising findings to your classes

For you, generalising the findings of research probably means looking at findings from previous work (be that scientific experiments, or the interventions used by other schools or in randomised controlled trials), and applying them to your own context. In other words, you are generalising from the sample and conclusions of one or more previous studies to your own learners.

There are certain factors that make a prior research phenomenon or finding easier to generalise to your own classroom:

- It is well established.
- It has a depth of literature supporting it, not just a few studies.
- It is practical, not speculative or purely theoretical.
- The mechanism of the effect/finding is understood.

- There is no obvious bias.
- It has been tested on learning materials similar to what is used in your own classroom.
- It has been tested on learners similar to your own (not, for example, just on neurotypical individuals if you are working with autistic learners).

Having made the point about learners similar to your own, the uniqueness of any group of learners can be overstated. Learning works in a fundamentally quite similar way in all people—we all have a working memory, long-term memory and so on—and brain cells function in the same way for all. Most theories of memory, thinking, motivation and so forth attempt to explain these processes in a way that applies universally, although the details will differ depending on what is being learned and by whom. Do you have a good, theory-based reason for thinking that your learners are different from those who were tested in the previous research? Some reasons that would make sense include:

- Age: metacognition develops as we get older, so strategies that require planning or reflection (for example) might not generalise from college or university students to young children.
- Expertise: some learning processes change as we move from being a beginner to an expert (of course, abilities also increase with age, on average). Consider, for example, the expertise reversal effect, discussed in Chapter 13. This shows that interventions that work well with novices could be counterproductive with more advanced pupils.
- Motivation: what motivates your learners, or those who have been studied? For example, strategies that are successful with self-motivated learners in clubs or evening classes might not generalise to mainstream school settings.

Other learner differences that are more dubious are the ideas that learners vary greatly depending on their gender, culture, race and so forth. In general, evidence for such variation is weak, and the commonalities tend to be much greater than the differences.

The educational system can also make a difference. Researchers who have studied programmes which provide one laptop or tablet for every learner have found considerable variation in terms of the outcomes across different programmes and countries.[2] The value for money of such technological investment has also been questioned; cognitive psychologists Henry Roediger and Mary Pyc have argued in favour of prioritising improvements to teaching and learning practices such as using retrieval practice (see Chapter 3), as these are inexpensive compared to new technology and have much stronger evidence behind them.[3]

Special educational needs naturally affect many educational processes, but even here there are similarities across learners—processes such as scaffolding and review are just as helpful for learners with additional needs.[4] However, it's worth noting that research studies may deliberately minimise the diversity of their sample in order to gain more consistent results, for example by excluding certain groups when recruiting participants.

Finally, the idea that learners can be categorised by simple preferences such as their 'learning style' or whether they are 'left- or right-brained' are widely considered to be myths (see From the research, below).

From the research

Key issue: is every learner unique? A common refrain among learners and teachers alike is that every learner is different, with the implication that our educational practices must cater for this. But is this actually true? And if so, do we need to teach children in multiple different ways?

What the research says: although many research fields (e.g. cognitive psychology, sociology, economics) tend to make a simplification that people are fundamentally quite similar and will react to pressures and stimuli in similar ways, it is clear that people differ in important ways, too. The study of individual differences

(continued)

(continued)

is a major branch of psychology, and two particular areas of focus are personality and ability.

Personality concerns traits such as extraversion and agreeableness that are usually assumed to be very enduring across the lifespan.[5] Such differences could affect how well learners engage with tasks—introverts may be less comfortable with unstructured group work, for example.

While there are clearly differences in learner ability, opinions vary as to why these exist. There may be some genetic factors at play, but it is also clear that experience and practice play major roles. While two people who attend an art class might be achieving at different levels by the end, does this mean that they have different innate ability? Perhaps, but it is also possible that one had a set of prior knowledge, experience and linguistic abilities that allowed them to get more out of the same lessons. More importantly, both learners are likely to be considerably more accomplished than a peer who has never been taught about art at all. While good teaching isn't always a leveller, all learners can make considerable gains when they receive skilled instruction which is pitched at the right level.

One particularly flimsy idea about individual differences—now largely rejected by mainstream education and psychology researchers alike—is the notion that people have different **learning styles** based on sensory modalities (visual, auditory and kinaesthetic being the most popular version). In practice, the best way to learn something depends mainly on the material or skill to be learned—nobody could learn to drive purely by listening to audiobooks, for example. What's more, it's much better to include multiple sensory experiences, rather than selecting a single one; successful driving instruction includes visual information about the road, auditory instructions from the tutor, and the kinaesthetic experience of using the controls. Where learners do express preferences—for example, preferring to learn visually—catering for these appears to make no difference to how successfully they learn.[6] Overall, this theory is considered a myth; trying to identify a learner's 'style' is a waste of time and may lead to counterproductive labelling.

Understanding the theory behind a change

To dig more deeply into the issue of where research can be generalised and where it should not be, we really need to understand why an effect has happened in a particular study.

The problem with a great deal of educational research is that it focuses on surface behaviours and outcomes, but the underlying reasons are open to speculation. We may observe that an intervention had an effect on a group of learners, but we don't always know why. Without understanding all of the variables that were at play in the situation, it's not possible to make an accurate judgement of whether it will work again in another setting.

For example, an intervention to introduce mind mapping to improve revision skills may be helpful with a group of learners who are doing ineffective revision or no revision at all. Generalising from this group to all learners could lead to the same strategy being tried with learners who are already revising effectively. In this situation, the intervention could actually make things worse—as mind mapping appears to be a less effective option than other revision strategies such as retrieval practice.[7]

Overall, then, we should try to to ensure three things when learning from the evidence base:

* That any proposed change/intervention is consistent with the evidence, and not biased by our assumptions.
* That we have given thought to how this evidence might generalise to our learners, and made adjustments accordingly.
* We have a clear theoretical rationale for why an intervention that has worked in another context should be beneficial in ours, too.

Research project: different groups of learners could react differently to an intervention, and something that works well in your class might not work everywhere. This could be an interesting area of investigation in itself, and identifying the limits of research-based teaching ideas is also useful preparation if you plan to share those ideas and experiences with others.

How to do it: focusing on the issue which you researched for the previous chapter's project or on another educational intervention that you consider useful for your own classes, prepare some notes on how it would generalise to other groups. Some questions to tackle might include:

- Would it apply to younger learners?
- Would it apply to learners with dyslexia? Or autism?
- Would the same principles apply to other topics/subject areas?
- Can we be sure that the effects of the intervention will be long lasting?

Write out two or three sentences on each of these points, being as critical and sceptical as possible. You can refer to any other context/group that is of interest.

As well as being a useful exercise in thinking about the limitations of any educational intervention, this sort of writing will be needed if you are going to write up the findings of a research project and submit it for publication, because these are the kind of points that researchers make in the 'discussion' section of their academic articles.

Concluding comments

Looking to research to provide a list of strategies may work some of the time, but if you don't understand why, there is a risk that a strategy may backfire. It's important to understand the principles of generalising from a sample that has been tested, and to consider any differences between our learners and those studied.

Some research may also be biased, but then, we are all biased—it's only human! And at times we have to accept certain things on the basis that they seem reasonable. However, it is well worth taking a questioning stance towards supposedly evidence-based strategies, even if they appear convincing and exciting.

We can also benefit from a deeper look at the research, and from considering the theory behind it. Understanding the how and why of research-based interventions puts you in a better position to know what will generalise to your context, and also facilitates evaluating any research that you read.

Further reading

A major review and synthesis of evidence-based research strategies was conducted by John Hattie and colleagues. You can read about these in Hattie's 'Visible learning for teachers' (2011, Routledge).

Discussion questions

- In terms of your confidence in generalising results from other research to your own learners, what matters most? Would you place more store on controlled laboratory research, for example, or would you rather focus on practitioner-led projects conducted in classrooms similar to your own?

- Imagine you did some research on a teaching strategy, and found that there hasn't been any research carried out in your particular setting or teaching subject. What would be the next best thing?

Notes

1 This is similar to political sampling. If you wanted to find out views of the public ahead of the next election, you couldn't just ask your friends.

The chances are that for various reasons, this non-random sample would give a biased result.

2 Ames, M. G. (2016). Learning consumption: Media, literacy, and the legacy of One Laptop per Child. *The Information Society*, 32(2), 85–97.
3 Roediger III, H. L., and Pyc, M. A. (2012). Inexpensive techniques to improve education: Applying cognitive psychology to enhance educational practice. *Journal of Applied Research in Memory and Cognition*, 1(4), 242–248.
4 Rix, J., and Sheehy, K. (2014). Nothing special: The everyday pedagogy of teaching. In L. Florian (Ed.) *The Sage handbook of special education, 2nd ed.* (pp. 459–474). London: Sage.
5 McCrae, R. R., and Costa Jr, P. T. (1999). A five-factor theory of personality. *Handbook of Personality: Theory and Research*, 2, 139–153.
6 Husmann, P. R., and O'Loughlin, V. D. (2018). Another nail in the coffin for learning styles? Disparities among undergraduate anatomy students' study strategies, class performance, and reported VARK learning styles. *Anatomical Sciences Education*, 12(1), 6–19.
7 Blunt, J. R., and Karpicke, J. D. (2014). Learning with retrieval-based concept mapping. *Journal of Educational Psychology*, 106(3), 849–858.

Using a research-based intervention in your classroom

Having taken away the key messages from the area of research that you have been studying and then given some thought to which messages generalise to your teaching context, you will, of course, be keen to start applying the ideas to your classroom! It's time to get stuck in—to actually try out an intervention based on a body of research in a way that you think will help your learners.

This chapter is about making gradual modifications to your own teaching practices in a way that follows the ideas and principles gleaned from research evidence, and the next chapter, Chapter 6, is about evaluating such an intervention. These chapters are *not* about conducting your own experiments or other elaborate research projects (where you gather data and then analyse and perhaps publish the findings); the various steps of that process are described in Part Two of this book.

Making direct changes

Applying research is about making changes to your teaching practice. Therefore, application of research has a direct link to pedagogy. Sometimes this might make you feel uncomfortable—you're already a trained teacher, so why should you change how you do things? Be reassured that this is in principle no different from trying out a new lesson idea or worksheet. In just the same way, you will try out a new and apparently worthwhile idea, and then reflect on the outcome. The difference is that these changes will be based on research evidence. Like tinkering with an engine to make it run better, this is part of a broader and continual process of implementing changes, evaluating and then making further changes as required.

It's important to remember here that we are not talking so much about 'doing research', but more about informing practice. As a professional, you may be expected (by professional teaching bodies, and perhaps parents and school management) to inform your teaching practice with evidence. It's now time to look in depth at how best to do that.

As suggested above, a gradual approach is likely to be sensible. Tempting though it is to bring in an exciting new technique (like Rebecca with her Technique Z, in Chapter 4), introducing changes cautiously, a little at a time, minimises the risk of unwelcome side effects. For example, perhaps you might find that although an idea for a new teaching strategy concords with the evidence, your pupils really hate doing it! You will want to find this out on a small scale—not after having re-written an entire topic to include it. You will also want to make changes cautiously to avoid jeopardising the good practice that is already a feature of your classroom.

As an analogy, think of a competent cook who is experimenting with new spices or herbs. He or she knows that these ingredients are used by the top chefs, and have the potential to transform a meal. However, it's also possible that recklessly pouring in lots of new spices without taking time to consider and evaluate previous changes would actually make their cooking a lot worse!

In short, the process of applying what you have learned from the research is to proceed in small steps, with considerable evaluation of progress (covered in the next chapter) and reflection along the way.

Specifying the intervention

If you have already followed the guidance and tasks presented in the foregoing chapters, and read research books or papers relevant to your own setting, then you may already have a clear idea in mind about what research-based intervention(s) you would like to try out with your own learners.

However, if not, here are some ideas which could apply to nearly every classroom:

Increasing the level of retrieval practice

Almost any lesson in any subject could vary the extent to which learners have to actively retrieve information or skills from memory. This could vary from a low to a high level, and there is strong evidence to suggest that this is an effective way of consolidating learning (see Chapter 3).

It needn't even be the case that learners have actually covered something before being quizzed on it. The pre-testing effect suggests that long-term retention is improved simply by asking questions before presenting the information.[1]

Improving the use of concrete examples

Concrete examples and links to the real world can make new concepts much easier to take in, but learners are rather poor at generating their own examples.[2] Teachers can add well-chosen examples to both presentation and practice of concept learning, ideally **interleaving** these to help learners develop an understanding of how concepts differ. For example, if presenting information about oxbow lakes, it would be useful to contrast these with examples of other types of lakes. In language, sentences with examples of a grammatical structure could be used, again contrasted with sentences where it is *not* used. Most teachers probably use too few examples; research suggests that a strategy of presenting two or more examples will be more beneficial than just one,[3] and that it can be more useful for learners to formulate an explanation of a process than to simply compare and contrast two examples.[4]

Varying the timing of when practice occurs.

There may well be an optimal time to practice new content or skills. According to the **spacing effect** (see From the research on p. 70), it's likely that increasing the time delay between initial learning and practice will boost attainment. How soon this should be done will depend on a number of factors, though, including the difficulty of the material and the strengths of the learners themselves. The teacher may be the best judge of how spacing should be implemented, ideally waiting until (based on prior experience) learners are likely to be on the cusp of forgetting, but have not actually done so yet.

Varying the balance of time between presenting new content and consolidation.

Courses and individual topics can vary widely in terms of the proportion of time devoted to presentation of new material, compared to that allocated to practice. In a university setting, it may be the case that most of the contact time is based around lectures with new content, with consolidation left up to the student. School pupils may be allocated some study time, but they typically have limited free time during the week for revision, and lack experience in revising effectively.

It may be worth experimenting with a faster pace of initial learning in schools, with periodic sessions devoted just to consolidation. Such a strategy would give you the chance to guide pupils' choice of revision strategies—something that the research suggests are typically very flawed![5]

From the research

Key issue: is it best to study something intensively, or space it out over time? Common sense might say that it would be best to repeat a practice session fairly soon, before learners have time to forget what they have learned. On the other hand, it also feels ineffective to practice something too soon—we may feel like we need a bit of time out before further practice. Can research shed light on how long we should wait before repeated practice?

What the research says: surprisingly, and counter to most people's intuition, leaving a longer gap before retrieval and/or consolidation seems to be highly beneficial when judged in terms of long-term retention.

A typical research study involves a study session, a variable delay before a practice session, and then a further delay before a final test. The time between the second practice session and the test is typically kept constant, and therefore what changes as part of the experiment is only one variable—the length of delay between the first and second study sessions:

```
STUDY 1..STUDY 2.............................TEST
STUDY 1.............STUDY 2.............................TEST
```

What numerous research studies have shown with a wide range of learning materials is that a larger delay tends to be beneficial. Indeed, there seems to be almost no limit to how much you can extend that initial delay before the increased space stops being beneficial and starts to be harmful. In one experiment, learners who had studied trivia facts were were tested with delays of up to a year.[6]

In practical terms, it is worth considering when learners will need to retrieve the information—for senior pupils, their exam date is a key part of the equation. If this is far away (e.g. for GCSE pupils at the beginning of Year 10), a long delay is likely to be beneficial. If it's sooner (e.g. pupils studying something for the first time in April with an exam coming up in May) then a shorter delay is essential—but it would still be best to space out the study sessions to an extent.

One final point is that spacing is unlikely to be helpful unless mastery has been achieved in the first learning session,[7] with numerous chances to retrieve the new learning as well as some tasks that involve transfer of facts or skills to novel scenarios. Leaving a long delay after a study session where the learners didn't really get what they were studying is likely to be unhelpful. But a brief delay (5–10 minutes) could still be more beneficial than immediate repetition.

General and specific

As can be seen from the examples above (and from the case study below), some research-based principles are general, applying to multiple situations. Other strategies are more subject specific. For example, a research-based strategy may only apply to materials in a small number of subjects, such as the use of a visual technique for explaining fractions in maths, or a method for teaching drawing. While it's tempting to look at a strategy that is successful in another subject and apply it to our own, it is also risky. In truth, we cannot really say that something is evidence-based if it has never been tried in our teaching domain.

Case study: the research-based school

Consider the following case of a school which aims for all aspects of teaching practice to be evidence-based. How well does this fit with the ideas of gradual and cautious change? Who is in charge of these changes, who is setting the agenda, and who gets to decide whether they have been a success or not?

> Lord Lyons Academy is a school which considers itself to be at the cutting edge of learning science in its educational approach and methods. Its stated goal is for all aspects of teaching practice to have a foundation of research evidence.
> The headteacher and school governors worked together over the whole of last summer to produce a booklet for staff. This lists over thirty 'evidence-based teaching practices', including recommendations for applying cognitive psychology research to maths and literacy, and for structuring pupil behaviour.

This school and its management show a keen engagement in research, and they will most likely foster an environment that makes it easier for teachers to both use research and experiment with their own research interests.

However, there are some flaws with simply providing a list of approved strategies. What works can be very context dependent, and may vary by age or subject. Additionally, handing out officially sanctioned strategies to staff will not, in itself, do much to boost either their theory-based understanding of those strategies, or their ability to keep themselves research informed on an ongoing basis. Ultimately, almost anything could be justified in terms of being evidence-based, and it's important for professionals to engage with the evidence themselves.

Putting it into practice

Now that you have selected an intervention (let's focus on one, for now, though of course you may have your sights set on more than one change—see the project on pp. 76–77), let's consider what to do next.

While many aspects of your preparation will of course depend on the specifics of what you are planning, there are certain steps that can be followed, each of which mimics the processes of the scientific method, helping you to translate the research idea into something that is classroom-ready:

Moving from the abstract to the concrete

First, an idea needs to be formulated in a way that is sufficiently concrete. What, for example, are the practical implications of the idea that some learners were more securely attached to their parents as infants? An idea about using schemas for learning or increasing pupils resilience may sound good, but what does it actually mean in practice?

In some cases (e.g. spacing) practical applications are relatively self-explanatory, but others are not. You may benefit from advice from a colleague or from a researcher in the particular area. Many research papers have some comments about applications towards the end (in the 'discussion' section of the paper) stating how the ideas could be applied, and in better papers these are usefully concrete and practical.

However, there may be some concepts that are simply too vague to apply in a classroom context, in which case it would be best to put the idea on the back burner and select an alternative that suggests a clear, practical intervention.

Translating the concrete idea to your learning context

Once you have worked through the practical implications of your idea, you still need to consider how it will apply to your specific subject. Educational examples that you come across are often aimed mainly at content-focused subjects like science and social sciences, and may be a bit harder to link to the skills and techniques taught across other parts of the curriculum, such as language, technology, sports or music.

In order to do this effectively, it can help to think through all of the stages of the teaching and learning process in your subject. Here are some of the major areas where research can be applied to the teacher's role—bear in mind that even if a concept or finding is irrelevant to many of these, it might make a critical difference to one or two areas:

- Lesson planning
- Course planning
- Materials/worksheet design
- Planning better starter tasks
- Planning better main tasks
- Planning better plenaries
- Motivating learners
- Managing pair work or group work
- Supporting vulnerable pupils
- Guiding learner note taking
- Guiding writing
- Modifying the demand of a task
- Improving learning habits
- Improving behaviour
- Improving humour and rapport
- Improving praise
- Improving feedback
- Improving mastery goals
- Planning homework

- Planning research projects
- Planning extra curricular experiences
- Planning cross-curricular learning
- Revision and review tasks

Hopefully this list of contexts will stimulate your thinking about how and when the idea can be applied in your subject. For example, if thinking about applying the spacing effect, it could be applied to homework (change the delay between lesson and homework?) or course planning (modify the termly schedule of lessons?) or projects (modify the timescale?) and various others, too . . . There's no need to change everything at once, and the intervention may work better in some contexts than others.

Specifying a lesson or series of lessons where you will trial the intervention

Finally, you will need to think of a specific concept or lesson in your subject where you can apply the idea. Again, on the basis of making gradual changes, a lesson or short series of lessons would be preferable to an entire course or topic. You might also choose to focus the change on a particular learner, one who needs additional support.

It might be best to choose a problematic area in your teaching, where you don't feel that you have been getting the learning experience quite right so far. That would make sense from the point of view that the largest impact is likely to occur in areas that are currently flawed. Alternatively, perhaps you'd rather try something new in a topic area where your lessons already go very well. This could also make sense, because it would allow you to get to grips with a new technique in a context where you have a lot of confidence with the material, with a view to later expanding the technique into trickier topics.

Often it may be best to try something out in a single lesson, and then evaluate it straight away. However, for some interventions, this may be impossible. For example, spacing—by its nature—has to be implemented over a period of time, usually requiring at least three sessions: a first study session, a second study session, and an assessment (although it's possible that these could fall within a single day or lesson, with short gaps in between). And even for techniques that could be applied just in one lesson, it might be hard to get enough feedback on its impact if you don't attempt it on more than one occasion.

Specifying tasks and materials

At an even more fine-grained level, you may need to integrate the research-based idea into a specific activity or piece of work.

One example might be the use of spacing in a literacy lesson. Specifying this even more, perhaps you might decide to apply the spacing effect to a particular list of vocabulary in the context of a spelling task, together with an activity where learners need to write sentences using the words in context. Spacing could be achieved by locating the presentation and spelling practice at the start of a 1-hour lesson, and the practice at the end. Alternatively, the spelling and practice task could be done on day one, and then repeated with less guidance the following day, with a spelling test a week later.

Research project: planning is a key aspect of being research-engaged. This chapter has focused on choosing and making a specific intervention; your next project is to plan a longer series of interventions by testing out multiple changes.

How to do it: note down your initial ideas on interventions that you would like to try. You could start with the four ideas listed near the start of this chapter. It may be helpful to think of a specific lesson/year group.

Now add a few more ideas to the list based on research evidence that you have read independently or based on the 'further reading' suggestions in this book—things that appeal to you, and which you would be interested in applying in your classroom.

It's worth thinking about practicality. Could these ideas be applied relatively quickly, with minimal costs in terms of workload? Could any of them backfire? Establish a list of things that you are keen to try out in the next 12 months (in order if possible), and a second list which are of genuine interest but for which there are obstacles to trying them in the near future. Going even more in-depth, you could begin to sketch up a schedule for which ideas you are going to try and when.

Finally, have a think about evaluation. How easy is it going to be to figure out whether these ideas have actually helped? You may need to try changes one at a time. Accurate, unbiased evaluation is the focus of the next chapter.

Concluding comments

This chapter has focused on several well-supported and flexible interventions that apply to any subject area, such as the spacing effect. Some readers will no doubt feel that a comprehensive list of evidence-based interventions would be helpful! However, as with the case study of Lord Lyons Academy, this may just become a checklist of 'approved' things to do, when in reality, there can't ever really be a definitive list, not least because research moves on all the time, and because what is effective is likely to depend on the context.

Nevertheless, there are numerous ideas that can be gleaned via the 'From the research' boxes in every chapter of the book, as well as from the suggested further reading. As long as you continue to critique new ideas and consider counter evidence, it would be well worth cautiously beginning to apply some of these to your practice, and to continually add to your 'to do' list of potential improvements.

Further reading

My own co-authored book, 'Psychology in the Classroom' by Marc Smith and Jonathan Firth (2018, Routledge) focuses on applying psychological evidence to all aspects of teaching practice. Each chapter takes an areas from the research—largely cognitive psychology, but also on areas such as motivation and self-regulated learning—and explains how it can be applied to planning, materials preparation, presentation of new concepts, homework and many other areas. Chapter 1 of the book focuses on memory, and on the spacing effect in particular.

Discussion questions

- How could you make use of the spacing effect with your learners? What constraints or deadlines would you have to consider?

- Have you ever been given a list of suggested teaching strategies to use, and if so, what was your experience of this?

- What is on your 'to do' list of future interventions, and which ones are nearest the top of the list in terms of priority?

Notes

1 Metcalfe, J. (2017). Learning from errors. *Annual Review of Psychology*, 68, 465–489.
2 Zamary, A., Rawson, K. A., and Dunlosky, J. (2016). How accurately can students evaluate the quality of self-generated examples of declarative concepts? Not well, and feedback does not help. *Learning and Instruction*, 46, 12–20.
3 Bauernschmidt, A. (2017). Guest post: Two examples are better than one. *Learning Scientists website*. Retrieved 20 December 2018 from http://www.learningscientists.org/blog/2017/5/30-1
4 Chin, D. B., Chi, M., and Schwartz, D. L. (2016). A comparison of two methods of active learning in physics: inventing a general solution versus compare and contrast. *Instructional Science*, 44(2), 177–195.

5 Hartwig, M. K., and Dunlosky, J. (2012). Study strategies of college students: Are self-testing and scheduling related to achievement?. *Psychonomic Bulletin & Review*, 19(1), 126–134.
6 Cepeda, N. J., Vul, E., Rohrer, D., Wixted, J. T., and Pashler, H. (2008). Spacing effects in learning a temporal ridgeline of optimal retention. *Psychological Science*, 19(11), 1095–1102.
7 Rawson, K. A., and Dunlosky, J. (2011). Optimizing schedules of retrieval practice for durable and efficient learning: How much is enough? *Journal of Experimental Psychology: General*, 140(3), 283–302.

6 | Evaluating your intervention

The previous chapter described how the research-informed teacher can use evidence to influence their own practice, interpreting a finding from the research in education or other related fields, and then adapting it to their own learning context. Of course, it's not enough just to implement a change—we also want to know whether it worked or not! It's possible that even an intervention that has a sound body of research supporting it might not work in all contexts.

However if an intervention does work as hoped, we need to be sure of this—and ready to take the next step. This chapter will consider how we draw accurate conclusions, and looks at areas where professional reflection alone is insufficient.

What are the key concepts?

Clearly we may accurately conclude that an intervention helped, or that it made no difference. However, there are two further possibilities to consider which we can borrow from medical research terminology: the false positive and false negative.

- It's possible that an intervention has had a positive effect on learners, but that we have failed to observe or measure it. For example, our homework quiz was beneficial for learning, but because none of the consolidated items were in the final exam, we see no difference in attainment between learners who did it and those who did not. Researchers call this scenario a **false negative**.

- It could be the case that we think the intervention has worked, but it actually did not—any change that we observe, such as behaviour or grades improving, may have been due to other factors. Researchers call this scenario a **false positive**.

We want to increase the chance of a correct conclusion (regardless of the direction), and minimise the chance of either a false positive or false negative (in statistics, these are often known by the less memorable names of 'type I and type II errors').

A false positive may result in our persisting with an intervention which is not actually doing learners any good, meaning that we are focusing time and effort on something pointless (remember 'learning styles' from Chapter 4?). A false negative, on the other hand, could mean that we fail to identify the benefits of something that did have real potential, and with which it would have been best to persist.

In order to avoid these outcomes, we need to think about how to evaluate an intervention—and how not to do so.

Case study: the self-report evaluation

Many interventions are evaluated in a fairly simplistic way, with little more than a short questionnaire asking participants whether they liked the change or not. In such circumstances, learners (or colleagues) may feel pressured into telling the teacher what they want to hear, or may simply not know whether it was beneficial. Consider the example below:

Agnes has been trying out a new form of Powerpoint with her Biology class. She is concerned that speaking over a slide that has a lot of text could overload their working memory, and is therefore showing slides that are largely pictorial, and

(continued)

(continued)

giving a verbal description from her notes. She then shares these notes with classes at the end of the lesson.

In order to find out how things are going since making this change, Agnes has asked each of them to fill in a short questionnaire. This asks questions like 'do you like the new style of lesson', and 'do you feel you are learning better than you were before?'. She emails it to all **60** of her A-Level students, and receives 14 responses.

What flaws are there from the example above? One is that learners' reports are likely to be *biased*. Imagine you are leaving a party, and the host says, 'did you have a good time?'. Most people would say 'yes' to that question—no matter what they were really thinking! Pupils may be more honest, particularly those who are academically well motivated and determined to get the best from their schooling, but they are also subject to **social desirability bias**—the social pressure to look good to the person who asks the question. Such questions may also be *leading*, that is, they prompt the learner as to what sort of answer is expected.

A second issue is that it relies on a learner's memory of what they did, and memory can be unreliable. They may remember a specific aspect of a lesson that they found annoying and give feedback on the basis of that, while forgetting many aspects that they enjoyed.

A further issue is that just because learners like something and feel that it is working, this doesn't mean it actually is. To put this another way, if learners had perfect insight into what works simply through their intuition, we wouldn't need to do any educational research at all—we could simply ask them what they want!

However, the reality is that learners don't always have a particularly sophisticated insight into learning, and their feedback on lessons are likely to be based around their preferences (did I enjoy it?) and their subjective impressions of what a good lesson is supposed to look like. To quote one article on learning preferences, "the fact people can be sorted based on their self-reported impressions about what works for them does not make them right about what works for them".[1]

Finally, a learner's current mood (perhaps they are feeling happy and relaxed, or perhaps they are tired and irritated and really want to leave rather than complete your questionnaire!) could potentially bias their response.

Effective self-report

How do we make self-report feedback from pupils more accurate? The key will be to tackle the flaws highlighted in the case study: social desirability bias, leading questions, misremembering, and misunderstandings/lack of insight:

Reducing bias

As noted above, there can be pressure to answer questionnaires in ways that put ourselves in a good light, for example by appearing to be a hardworking student, or by avoiding negative feedback in case it leads to unpleasant consequences. One part of dealing with this issue is to use an anonymous system. It's also important that the pupils know and believe that it really is anonymous (they may be suspicious about this!), for example by soliciting responses that have no handwriting on, using a response box rather than gathering in sheets personally, or using an online form.

Asking very specific, factual questions, such as 'How long did this task take?' will also help to reduce this bias, in contrast to questions about how well the participant liked or disliked the intervention. It's also best to avoid questions that ask learners to judge a lesson or intervention holistically—again, being specific (for example, 'was the Powerpoint too long, in your view') makes the judgement more reliable.

Leading questions

Some questions may imply that a certain answer is desired or expected, biasing respondents away from other possible responses. Some even make a negative response next to impossible! There are many types; one of the most problematic is the type of question that asks for agreement, such as 'Do you agree that the class behaved better in today's lesson?'. Such questions make it easier for respondents to say 'yes' than 'no'. An alternative would be to use a more neutral question or statement, such as 'How well behaved were the class today?' or 'Agree/disagree: the class were well behaved today'.

Similarly, a double-barrelled question forces learners into a choice where they may not actually agree with either option. One example would be, 'did you like the new style of lesson or the old style of lesson?'. Such questions are best avoided.

Addressing memory and mood

As noted above, learners may misremember their lesson, and consequently feed back only on selective details. One way is to integrate questions naturally into tasks, resulting in a much tighter feedback loop. For example, a homework task which involves reading a text and answering questions could include a final question or two on evaluative/metacognitive issues, for example, 'On a scale of 1–10, how useful did you find this task', or 'Predict what percentage you would get if you were tested on this topic tomorrow'. Note that if connected to homework, it might not be possible to make responses anonymous.

Regarding mood, we all recognise that this varies from time to time. In order to minimise the bias that this may lead to, we could ask them for feedback on more than one occasion. Again, connecting this to homework may allow regular sampling to minimise one-off days where they are feeling down, but on the other hand, it may come with its own biases—perhaps they feel more (or less) relaxed at home than they do at school. Therefore a question will ideally be asked more than once, and in different settings.

Lack of insight

Finally, how do we tackle the issue that a learner simply might not know what works for them? There are numerous examples throughout this book of how people's beliefs about learning are flawed, and we can't assume that a new intervention has worked just because learners think they have or have not learned well (or, indeed, because the teacher thinks so).

The section below discusses other forms of evidence that might be used to indicate how well pupils have learned, but it's also useful to remember (as discussed in previous chapters) that learners' estimates of their progress are more accurate after a delay[2] or after a quiz[3]—and best of all after a delayed quiz. So the best time to ask them to assess their learning after an intervention or change might be after doing a class test, a week or two after the learning itself.

Naturally occurring evidence

Although there are ways of improving self-report evaluations, asking learners about their lesson is still fundamentally quite subjective. There are, however, many other forms of evidence that a teacher can use instead of (or in addition to) direct questioning of the learners. These don't need to involve something additional, outside of normal classroom practice. Indeed, it will often be best to use sources of evidence that are already part of the normal practice and procedures of the classroom, as these will be authentic. Examples include:

Scores on tests

There is no need to worry about designing a valid way of measuring changes to achievement if you can use tests and quizzes that were part of your classroom practice before the intervention. These are inherently valid! Scores on tests after an intervention could be compared to other classes, or to groups from previous years. However, you may want to find ways to ensure that the groups are comparable, such as by finding out their marks in other subjects (it might just so happen that you have an especially talented group this year, meaning that higher test scores would not be due to your intervention—a false positive). Another way to ensure scores are comparable would be to look at test scores from the same group before and after your intervention, again using previous years' marks for comparison.

Features of pupil work

Some features of classwork could be a form of data. For example, are the learners' essays more detailed? Do they write with more enthusiasm and confidence? Many of these things could allow you to make a simple comparison between a lesson where you used an intervention and one where you did not. A simple comparison of the length in words of pupils' essays with/without the intervention would be one such way—though other variables such as the amount of time they are given to work on the essay would have to be kept constant in order to make a fair comparison (see Chapter 9 for more on controlling variables). Also, you need to give some thought to what a change means. A shorter essay might imply that pupils were less engaged, but it could also mean that they spent more time thinking about and discussing the topic, and less time writing about it.

Behavioural signs of enjoyment

Aspects of pupils' behaviour could be assessed for signs that they are enjoying themselves, rather than using a questionnaire to ask them about their feelings. For example, do they put their hands up more than in the past? Do they come to class more punctually? Is behaviour better in the class? Such methods can be helpful in tackling the mis-match between what people say and what they do.

Some ways of recording this might already be part of your daily practice—perhaps you record late-comings in a mark book, for example— meaning that you can make a before and after comparison using authentic, naturally occurring data.

From the research

Key issue: the case study presented an example where learners reported liking an intervention. Is this not a beneficial end in itself? If learners are positive about a change and enjoy what they are doing, might this not have a knock-on effect on their learning or other areas of school? In short, how important is it that learners enjoy learning?

What the research says: research into motivation and memory shows that children who are engaged and happy learn better. We remember better if we are curious and motivated,[4] and we generally learn best if relaxed and not stressed (stress can actually reduce the number of neurons in the hippocampus, a brain area essential for forming new memories).[5]

Having said that, effective interventions are not always going to be pleasant, and sometimes learning is hard work. Interventions such as spacing and retrieval practice are often termed 'desirable difficulties'—things that make new learning harder, but are helpful overall.[6]

The reality is, though, that pupils often love a challenge if it appears to be meaningful, particularly if it fits with their sense of social belonging and identity, and if they feel that the challenge was freely chosen (see also Chapter 15).[7] Learners are not necessarily motivated by making things easier or pleasant in the here and now—consider the satisfaction that some people get from a really tough workout in the gym. Instead, the strongest motivating factors are a sense of competence, a sense of belonging and the idea that choices are our own.

There do appear to be cultural differences in how effort is viewed. In her book 'CleverLands', Lucy Crehan investigates the approaches of some of the world's highest performing education system. She concludes that contrary to the stereotype, countries such as Singapore and China don't succeed because they are highly controlling of pupils, but because their expectations

(continued)

(continued)

were very high. Pupils are not streamed or divided by attainment prior to age 15, and there is an assumption that high achievement depends on hard work.

The way that learners do or do not identify with hard work and a deep, critical approach to learning also depends on their social identity.[8] Do they see themselves as a learner? Is this a subject that feels like their kind of thing, and is it leading anywhere? And does the school as a whole foster a culture of engagement, curiosity and focused academic effort? These contextual factors will all affect whether a learner sees effort as worthwhile, or as something to be avoided.

Flawed evaluation

Even when the issues discussed so far in this chapter have been considered and accounted for, there is a possibility that your own evaluation of the change/intervention may be flawed in some way, leading to a false positive or false negative.

Perhaps most likely is the false positive—through enthusiasm for a change that seems to fit the research evidence, the teacher mistakenly thinks that there is a real and worthwhile benefit. While this may be inevitable to a certain extent (we can never be entirely free of bias!), there are three key ways of tackling it:

- Attempt to **triangulate** data by adding an additional source of feedback from among the ideas on pp. 85–86 so that you are not getting information just from a single source.

- Continue to keep records and conduct further evaluation periodically, not just at the start.

- Work with colleagues to trial the same interventions in their classes—often it is at the point where researchers try to roll an idea out on a larger scale that certain flaws become clear.

Overall, it is valuable to be open to the possibility that your new idea for an improvement to classroom practice is not all that you hoped. A negative result can be just as useful as a positive one—indeed, it may save you a lot of time if you find that a popular new pedagogical strategy doesn't actually make any difference.

Likewise, of course, some aspects of your current practice that you consider to be evidence-informed may turn out to have major limitations. As teachers, our classroom style is often very tied up with identity—we like to be thought of as good and effective and it's quite threatening to think that things we have done for years might be flawed. However, rather like finding out that something that you regularly eat is actually unhealthy, it may be bad news, but it's also useful to know about it sooner rather than later. More broadly, your engagement with research may mean that any idea you are implementing today will be tomorrow's baseline measure. In the world of medicine, new drugs are not usually compared to a placebo but to the best current treatment. In a similar way, you will make improvements, read the research further and then try to make things better still. With such a programme of continual professional improvement, nothing is left unexamined over the long run.

Research project: what factors make learners better able to judge their own learning and motivation? Two suggestions are made above—delaying the judgement, and using a test. Why not investigate whether pupils' judgements of their own learning are accurate in your context. After all, if learners have a flawed perception of their own learning, it's not just a problem for your research—it's also an issue that might lead to their making bad study choices, such as spending too little time revising, or focusing on the wrong material.

How to do it: the key aspect of such a study will be to have data available to you on how the pupils' learning is progressing, and to ask them at some point to make estimates of this. As suggested earlier, this could be made more reliable by asking the question

(continued)

(continued)

on more than one occasion, to allow for shifts in mood. A simple question such as 'predict your percentage score on the next test' could be answered once a week, sometimes within a homework task and other times in class.

This doesn't need to be a research study as such (although it could be—but first read up on research ethics in Chapter 8); instead, it can just be an everyday part of your classroom practice, raising awareness of these issues among your learners and providing useful feedback for you as the teacher.

Once you start to gather this information, you could regularly calculate the correlation between pupil estimates on the one hand and their test scores on the other, giving them feedback where appropriate. Even without taking any further action you could investigate patterns in the data—for example, perhaps learners' predictions rise as their understanding improves, or fall as the test approaches. Any such findings would have implications for how learners could be better prepared to understand their own learning, and could stimulate a more in-depth research project for you.

Concluding comments

The issues covered in this chapter and the previous one comprise a process that can—and arguably should—form the basis of evidence-based professional practice. Changes can be informed by evidence, but it is still important to be sceptical, and to find accurate ways of investigating their impact. While learners' views are important, there are, as we have seen, multiple factors that could bias self-report data such as responses to in-class questionnaires. This chapter has explored ways of improving such data, as well as using data from existing sources in order to evaluate changes in your classroom practices.

Finally, it's worth acknowledging that data is not the same as reflection. Teachers are often encouraged to be reflective practitioners, following a research tradition dating back to John Dewey. This makes good sense—we don't want teachers just to continue repeating the same mistakes, but instead to engage in a cycle of continuous improvement. However, just as with our learners when they answer questionnaires, teachers do not always have full and unbiased awareness of whether a practice worked or not. The use of objective evidence has the potential to help the process of reflection.

Further reading

Crehan's 'CleverLands' (2018, Unbound Press), mentioned on p. 87 is a fascinating and stereotype-busting insight into what makes the school systems in some countries highly successful. It may well provide ideas for the kind of changes you would like to see in your own context.

In terms of reflecting on our own learning as teachers, 'The reflective practitioner: How professionals think in action' by Donald Schön is a classic. Still, given the points made in this chapter, it might be best read and analysed in light of modern research into metacognition, such as the 2013 article by Robert Bjork and colleagues entitled 'Self-regulated learning: Beliefs, techniques, and illusions', in the journal *Annual Review of Psychology*. There is no disputing the importance of teachers being reflective and learning from their own practice, but there are some interesting questions to ask about how illusions and misconceptions about learning might interfere with this process.

Discussion questions

- Think of a feedback questionnaire that you have answered recently, for example, after a conference or in-service training event. Do you think that it give you the opportunity to fully and clearly state your opinion? Do you think your opinion was typical of others in the session?

- Why might it be easier for a learner to accurately judge their own learning after a delay or a test?

- In your experience, what factors affect whether a learner enjoys hard work? Why do some give up more easily than others?

Notes

1 Pashler, H., Bjork, R., McDaniel, M., and Rohrer, D. (2015). Comment on Sternberg's review of Zhang. *American Journal of Psychology*, 128, 122–125 (123).

2 Nelson, T. O., and Dunlosky, J. (1991). When people's judgments of learning (JOLs) are extremely accurate at predicting subsequent recall: The "delayed-JOL effect". *Psychological Science*, 2(4), 267–271.

3 Roediger III, H. L., Putnam, A. L., and Smith, M. A. (2011). Ten benefits of testing and their applications to educational practice. In *Psychology of learning and motivation*, Vol. 55 (pp. 1–36). New York: Academic Press.

4 Kang, M. J., Hsu, M., Krajbich, I. M., Loewenstein, G., McClure, S. M., Wang, J. T. Y., and Camerer, C. F. (2009). The wick in the candle of learning: Epistemic curiosity activates reward circuitry and enhances memory. *Psychological Science*, 20(8), 963–973.

5 McEwen, B. S., and Sapolsky, R. M. (1995). Stress and cognitive function. *Current Opinion in Neurobiology*, 5(2), 205–216.

6 Bjork, E.L. and Bjork, R.A. (2011). Making things hard on yourself, but in a good way: Creating desirable difficulties to enhance learning. In Gernsbacher, M.A., Pew, R.W., Hough, L.M. and Pomeranz, J.R. (Eds). *Psychology and the real world: Essays illustrating fundamental contributions to society* (pp. 56–64). New York: Worth Publishers.

7 Ryan, R. M., and Deci, E. L. (2017). *Self-determination theory: Basic psychological needs in motivation, development, and wellness*. London: Guilford Publications.

8 Smyth, L., Mavor, K. I., Platow, M. J., Grace, D. M., and Reynolds, K. J. (2015). Discipline social identification, study norms and learning approach in university students. *Educational Psychology*, 35(1), 53–72.

PART 2

The teacher as researcher

Once you begin to engage more with research evidence, you may find that elements of your thinking about education change. Just asking questions such as 'how does this work?' or 'is there any evidence that this is effective?' can be transformational over time. More and more, you will begin to explore areas of research that impact on all aspect of your teaching and professional life, and, as time goes on, find that it is having an influence on all aspects of practice.

For some of us, applying research evidence to inform classroom choices is enough, at least for now. However, published research evidence can't answer every question you might have. Too much about your practice is unique and context-specific, and there are some areas where the existing research is inadequate, or where you might not have faith in it for various reasons. Ok, you might think, so research has shown that Technique Z works for first grade science pupils in America, but will it work for my class? Whether you are a new teacher or several decades in, you may decide the time has come to answer these questions for yourself by conducting your own studies.

The phenomenon of teachers conducting their own research has increasingly become part of the teacher education process; many teachers complete practical research projects for the dissertation of a Master's course or doctorate, and some do so at an earlier stage too. Although such projects can form part of structured courses, they can also help build the skills for later autonomous research. A bit like becoming a competent teacher, there comes a point where you take ownership and set the objectives for yourself, and where it is no longer down to your mentors to show you what to do. At that point, using and conducting research becomes an integral part of your professional development.

This part of the book will guide you through the process of going from research informed to becoming a teacher-researcher. It will cover generating a research question and planning a study (Chapter 7), explain the principles of research ethics (Chapter 8), and explain research variables and control (Chapter 9). We will look at correlation studies (Chapter 10), and qualitative and quantitative methods (Chapters 11–12) for data gathering. Finally, this part also explores research that is based in but not based on education, such as pupil projects and research into your subject specialism (Chapter 13).

The next step

Up until now, this book has focused largely on how and why a teacher might engage with research, and provided guidance on making your classroom practice evidence-informed.

Now, it's time to consider the next step—actually generating some of that evidence yourself.

Am I really doing research?

Multiple terms are used for the classroom-based investigations conducted by teachers and other practitioners. They are frequently described as 'action research', or as 'practitioner enquiry', and it is perfectly fine to use either of these terms.

However, it could be argued that different terminology implies that teachers' research projects are different in scope or quality from the research conducted by university-based researchers. Perhaps if a teacher is conducting a research project, it should just be called 'research'? You might want to consider the following points and counter-arguments before you decide how you feel about this:

- It's better to call it 'practitioner enquiry', because I am a practitioner (teacher), not a researcher. → Yes, you are a practitioner who intends to use this in practice, but so are many university-based researchers: most teach as well as conducting research.

- The research is done in a school. → Many research studies are done in schools, including the work of prominent cognitive scientists. Others are undertaken in universities, or with the general public. The target population studied is not a defining factor in how we define a piece of research.

- The research only applies to my context. → It is as hard to generalise your classroom-based findings to a lab setting as it is to do the reverse. As we have seen, most studies are only conducted in a single setting, and this doesn't mean that the findings are any less valid.

- I intend to use the findings to make changes to my practice. → This just means that the research is applied. It's possible to make a rough distinction between applied and theoretical research; again, a lot of research by university researchers into areas like memory and health is applied, and intended to affect the actions of people in everyday life.

- I already have a personal relationship with the learners, possibly biasing the findings. → Again, this is common in universities too, because many researchers conduct investigations involving their own students as participants. It doesn't necessarily invalidate the findings, but it is necessary to report this aspect of the methodology and what the implications might be.

- My project is too small-scale to count as proper research, so I wouldn't share it or expect others to act on the basis of the findings. → If your study is too small-scale for the findings to be valid, then nobody should be acting on the findings, yourself included. However, it can still function as a useful **pilot study**, that is, a small-scale investigation used to help develop methodology and better specify research variables; again, this is commonly done by university-based researchers too.

- I'm not going to analyse it statistically. → If we don't use statistical analysis, then we don't really know what we've found or what the implications might be. As with the previous point, it would be unwise for anyone, the practitioner included, to act on incomplete information.

As can be seen, many of the potential criticisms that could be made of teacher-led research projects are also true of many 'proper' research studies. The fact that it is run by a teacher and in a classroom is of less importance than how well the study is done. After all, a university researcher could do exactly the same thing that you are doing.

If other researchers wouldn't do what you plan to do because your plan is flawed, then it would be a good idea for you to address those flaws. For example, it's worth asking whether it's ok for you to skip certain features that would increase the reliability or validity of studies published in major journals. If published studies typically use 100+ participants and you intend to test a class of 15, are you actually going to get good data? And if not, will the findings tell you anything useful? On the other hand, if your study is done in a reliable way, then arguably it is 'research', even if you are not a university academic with a PhD. What you do matters more than who you are!

There is often a trade-off between realism and control in research. Laboratory experiments, of the kind that are popular in university psychology departments, have a high level of control over the surroundings, materials and participants. However, this comes at a cost—more tightly controlled studies have lower *ecological validity*, that is to say, they are less true to life. Don't lose sight of the fact that although your research may have flaws and be somewhat messier (in terms of control of variables) than published studies that you read, its authenticity is a major advantage,[1] and as such, it may well be of interest to others.

Perhaps the main thing that would make you define your work as 'practitioner enquiry' is a combination of the factors above, with the project forming a loop of ongoing professional improvement. Rather like the process described in Chapters 5–6, you intend to gather data on pupil or teacher participants, analyse it, and immediately use it in ways that will benefit those participants. You can, of course, use any terminology that you like to describe what you do, but it's important not to forget that well-run teacher-led research projects are worthwhile in themselves, and the findings may be worth sharing more broadly.

Avoiding bias

Enthusiasm for conducting research on a teaching technique or theory often goes hand in hand with enthusiasm for that idea itself. This can mean that many teachers have largely decided what they think the outcome of a study will be before they even gather any data. It is worth pausing to think about what the point of such a study would be. Perhaps the research literature is already clear, and there is universal or near-universal agreement—a particular intervention is effective (or it isn't). In this case, a small-scale school-based study isn't going to add very much to it. Or perhaps this area is a fad or trend, a currently-fashionable idea which over the long term will be rejected as not worth the time and effort.

In addition, remember the points about confirmation bias made in Chapter 4. Try asking yourself how you would react to a negative finding—are you just as willing to find and publish a flaw or limitation with the idea or theory as to support it? If not, it's possible that your emotional attachment to the research area could cloud your judgement! Remember that in order to best serve our learners, we need to be finding out truths about learning and behaviour, not simply supporting the popular theory of the day.[2]

Methodology

As you will have seen from your reading, there are many ways of conducting research and gathering data. It needn't involve questionnaires (arguably the staple of the novice educational researcher). The coming chapters will explore many of the options; to briefly preview these, we will look at:

* Correlation studies
* Observational research
* Interviews
* Questionnaire-based surveys
* Focus groups
* Experiments using tasks and tests

Case study: variation in modern language questioning

This case is based around variation theory—the idea that individual differences between learners can be explained by understanding how and why different learners focus their attention on different features from one another. For example, some language learners may focus on surface features such as the sound of a word or what it reminds them of, and fail to pay attention to a deeper grammatical principle:

> Hartesh wants to apply variation theory to his modern languages class. He has read that teachers can learn from variation theory to guide their questioning and the examples that they present. He has also learned from research into interleaving that it is sometimes beneficial for learners to see multiple examples of the same type (at the start of the learning process, or when the examples are very different) and sometimes beneficial to see multiple different examples (after initial learning has occurred, or when differences between examples are subtle).
>
> However, Hartesh has identified a flaw in the research literature—nearly all of it is conducted on university students, and most relates to new learning of unfamiliar material. In contrast, most of his classroom practice with teenaged pupils involves building on prior learning.
>
> In order to test whether variation will help his classes, Hartesh decides to prepare two sets of questions which he or another teacher can ask—one which shows many examples of a single grammatical feature, and one which has a mixture of different types of structure for learners to categorise. On the basis of the research evidence about difficulty, he predicts that varied examples will be useful for his more advanced pupils, while multiple similar examples will be useful for beginners.

(continued)

(continued)

The research project that Hartesh is undertaking is a good example of how research ideas can be applied to the classroom, and also shows how flaws in existing evidence can stimulate new research projects. Published psychology studies into memory and learning are commonly conducted on university students, making it hard to generalise to younger learners who may be different in various ways such as their breadth of vocabulary, motivation and prior learning (see Chapter 4). Such studies also tend to use novel material; this means that prior learning does not confound the results, but also, again, makes the conclusions harder to generalise to real classroom contexts.

A research aim and question

As the case study illustrates, you will at some point move from a general area of interest to a specific *aim*—what it is that you intend to achieve or find out. However, this should really just be pencilled in at the early stage. Consider it a rough sketch of the area that you'd like to find out more about, or the problem that you'd like to solve. If you are building on an intervention as described in previous chapters, you have a real head start here—you have already read a lot of relevant research, and by implementing it in your school, you will have raised new issues and problems that are worth investigating. Otherwise, it is important to read up on the background to the area, and begin to get an idea of what the main areas of debate are.

You will also be informed by your own needs or those of your learners. Typically, the aim will focus on a practical problem of some kind. For example, perhaps you want to find something out, such as how to plan more effective classes, how to ensure that all pupils do their homework, how to engage parents, or how to help struggling readers. You may have a technical aim, such as improving your use of Powerpoint, or making research projects both fun and worthwhile.

One example aim could be:

The aim of the study is to find whether the timing of practice affects children's learning of spelling.

Your aim can then be formulated into a more specific statement or *research question*, which starts to focus in on the particular idea that you have. For example:

Does spacing out spelling practice improve performance on spelling tests?

Note that the question above could just as easily be worded as an aim/objective statement ('The study will try to find out whether spacing out of spelling tests improves spelling performance') and the aims could be formulated as questions! The key difference between the aim and the research question is not its grammatical wording, but its breadth: the aim is broader and talks about the purpose of the research, while the question asks something specific that can be answered by your research findings.

While most teachers' research questions tend to focus on areas relevant to practice, you may choose a question that is particular to scholarship in your teaching subject, for example about cutting-edge research into an area of History, Philosophy or Physics. That's fine too!

It's a good idea to be as specific as possible with your question—who does it relate to? What intervention, if any, will be used? So the above research question could be reformulated:

Does splitting spelling test practice sessions into two shorter sessions spaced out by one week improve performance on spelling tests for Year 5 pupils?

Questions like the one above invite yes-or-no answers which is ideal for a quantitative (data-based) study, while for qualitative research, you may prefer to begin a question with words like 'how' or 'what', therefore leading you to investigate more complex and varied responses (see Chapters 11–12). However, it should still be specific. For example:

What are the factors that lead inexperienced primary school teachers to engage in the reading of journal articles?

Later, you will use the question as the basis for a research hypothesis which makes a prediction of the findings. This is discussed in the next section.

Planning

For any lengthy research project, it is helpful—even essential—to make a detailed plan of action at the start. This section describes the main steps that you might include in your plan. It's a good idea to write down your ideas for all of these stages, and to keep earlier versions rather than replacing them:

Brainstorming aims and research questions

What is it about classroom learning or behaviour that you'd most like to investigate? What issues are there in your own context that you find troubling, or where you are dubious about the effectiveness of mainstream practice? Perhaps there are aspects of your teaching on which you have received criticism during peer observations. For example, if you've been told that your classroom questioning needs to improve, this would be the ideal focus for a research project (and it's certainly worth asking—what evidence is there that the criticism was justified?!).

Finding suitable guidance

Who is the expert in this field? Is there anyone local, or could you email a researcher from another country with some quick queries? Closer to home, are there one or more other teacher-researchers who might collaborate with you on the project—perhaps people who have already been engaging with the evidence on this area for years, or who have research skills which complement your own?

Break down the research into sub-projects

What specific things do you need to do? Identify the main tasks that need to be completed. Then divide each of these into sub-projects. For example, data analysis can be subdivided: initial coding, entering data into a format for analysis (e.g. into a spreadsheet), running statistical tests, and analysing the outcome of those tests. Data gathering may also involve several tasks.

Establish a timeline

As noted in Chapter 2, the issue of having enough time could be reframed in terms of how many weeks or years you would need to find the required number of free hours for your research project. It doesn't matter terribly much whether you can free up half an hour or half a day each a week—all that changes is how quickly you will complete your tasks. For example, if a project will take 50 hours and you have an hour free per week, then it will take around a year. If you have four hours free per week, then you can do the same project in three months, with the same end result.

Identify any training needs

Do you need to find out more about literature reviewing? Statistical analysis? Questionnaire design? Time management and planning? As with your background research, you can draw on the help of knowledgeable colleagues and other contacts. Some projects may require a specialist training programme. Start to develop links at your local HE institute; some may be willing to allow you to audit research methodology modules in exchange for forming research links or hosting student teachers.

Read the background research

Any study will be more meaningful if founded on a thorough review of current research literature. It's important for your reading to include at least some current findings—what is the point in testing a theory that was debunked years ago? Pay particular attention to the last few paragraphs of each article, where an author often says something like 'It was unclear why x happened. Future research will need to address . . .'.

It's possible to fall down a rabbit hole in terms of background research—there's no obvious end point when you have read enough. For an initial project, set yourself a target for the early stage of your reading, perhaps ten papers including review articles and book chapters which provide overviews. You can always look at more papers later on. Spend some time figuring out which are the most useful ones to look at (taking advice if necessary). Avoid spending a lot of time on unfocused browsing through links, blogs or databases. Instead, have a goal, and ensure that you have moved closer towards that goal by the end of any allocated research time.

Specifying a hypothesis

Having established a specific research question, it is good practice to formulate this into a **research hypothesis**—a statement that predicts what will happen as the result of a change, or of the relationship between two variables. This will be informed by your reading.

For example, you could predict that when you do one thing (x), it will result in a particular outcome (y). Better still, the hypothesis will refer to the theoretical rationale, for example: 'if theory x is correct, x will result in y. If it is incorrect, x will not result in y'. Note that a *two-tailed hypothesis* doesn't state the direction of the difference, i.e. whether scores will rise or fall because of a change or intervention. It is best to predict a direction if you can; this is called a one-tailed hypothesis, for example:

Two-tailed hypothesis: giving pupils more planning time will affect the quality of their essays.

One-tailed hypothesis: pupils who are given 20 minutes of planning time will write better essays than those who are given five minutes of planning time.

The latter example is also more specific; it's best to specify (or 'operationalise') what the difference(s) there will be between different groups in your study.

Have a strategy for data analysis in place

All too often, inexperienced researchers gather a set of data and then ask 'now what?'. Don't let this be you! Your plan should include a detailed strategy for how the data will be gathered, summarised, analysed, and presented. You should also consider secure data storage, and ensure that all of your research practices are GDPR compliant.

One of the simplest ways to prepare would be to use fictional data and run a practice analysis. This will give you an idea of what your data might look like, what techniques you might use to analyse it, what problems could occur, and what tables, graphs or charts (if any) you could use to present the findings.

Better still, run a full pilot study of the methodology with a much smaller sample. This will allow you to fully understand the data analysis and storage implications, and make any changes necessary before running the full study.

From the research

<u>Key issue</u>: what kind of goals are the most motivating? Is it best to aim high and have a clear idea of the direction of travel, or is a distant target likely to be daunting for the novice teacher-researcher?

<u>What the research says</u>: a goal is the objective that we intend to reach through an action or series of actions. Setting goals is thought to make people more persistent, because consciously stating the goal guides a person's later attention and efforts.[3]

(continued)

(continued)

According to researchers Gary Latham and Edwin Locke, certain things make a person more likely to work towards a goal, specifically the perceived importance of the goal to them as an individual, the amount of satisfaction which they think they will get from achieving it, and their perceived ability to achieve the required steps. In contrast to some areas of social behaviour, there does not seem to be much variation in this across age, sex, or culture.[4]

Furthermore, Latham and Locke argue that the way a goal is phrased can affect how likely it is to be fulfilled. A goal should be phrased in a positive and active way (e.g. 'pass my exam' rather than 'avoid failing my exam'). Counterintuitively, it also helps if a goal is quite difficult (trivial goals seem to be less motivating), and expressed publicly, so that others know that you are working towards it. It is best if the goal can be specific, although as noted earlier, this can be difficult in the early stages of a research project.

A related issue is the question of whether to have a goal with multiple parts or a single goal. In the realm of health and sports, some researchers have studied the use of 'multicomponent goals' and found them more effective than working towards a single goal, although it is hard to say whether this can generalise to goals for research projects. It may be best to show some flexibility in goal setting, stating them clearly at the start, but modifying them as time goes on.

The stages of research

Establishing a timeline for your research project helps to make your goals more specific, providing detail and timings, while still recognising that some of these details may need to change as things progress. Setting out a timeline would be considered an essential early stage of a research-based degree, and for good reason: there is a real benefit to making a clear statement of what you want to do, and how you intend to get there, as it facilitates reflection on the plan and helps you to get feedback and identify flaws.

Having established the tasks and sub-projects, draft up a timeline that estimates how long these would take, and allocates time to each. A Gantt chart or spreadsheet will be helpful, here. Some of the main stages of the research process to include in your timeline are:[5]

Further investigation of background research and theories

Although often treated as the beginning stage of research, it's important to continue with your background reading as the project progresses, as any additional findings could inform planning of the next stage of your research and/or could be included in a research write-up. Allocate at least 20% of your time to this task.

Collecting data

You will plan to gather data in some form. For some projects, this may not differ greatly from the kind of naturally-occurring evidence dis-cussed in Chapter 6—pupil test scores, class behavioural records, school observation forms and the like. In other cases, you will need to find or develop a suitable data gathering procedure based around interviews, experiments, observations, and so forth.

Analysing the data

Don't forget to plan for the data analysis stage. Do you already have the skills to do this, or could it be done in collaboration with a co-researcher? And are you clear what kind of data you will gather? Understanding this at an early stage will help you to plan both for the amount of time data analysis will need, and for developing any skills required. For statistics, it's also worth bearing in mind that for any extensive set of data, it is usually necessary to use statistical software. There are books and web-sites which can guide you to the use of data analysis software, and you could learn by working together with a colleague.

Reporting results (optional)

You may wish to give some thought to what forums (if any) you will use to share your findings. Will this take place in school, via blogs, or will you try to publish your work? Some journals and magazines will publish pilot studies, plans, or projects that are still in progress. In any case, a considerable amount of time should be allocated to the writing process.

Taking informed action

As discussed earlier, you may choose not to act on the results of your research study for various reasons. Perhaps the sample was so small that the results are unreliable and you wish to treat the study as a pilot, or you found something very unexpected that appears to conflict with established research and you would therefore like to investigate further before taking action. Ultimately however, teacher-research is usually motivated by a desire to change what we do in the classroom. Does this part of my current practice work well, and if not, how could I change it for the better? It's useful to consider at planning stage how and when you might make these changes. Perhaps, for example, you plan to carry out a research project over one year, and make changes (if appropriate) based on the outcome the following year.

Research project: naturally, the project for this chapter is to draw out a detailed, specific research plan! Planning is an undervalued aspect of research; it's important to think a plan through and to make a realistic allocation of time.

How to do it: you may already be familiar with planning tools and software, but if not, a spreadsheet can work just as well. Put each of the stages listed in the previous part into the first column, and then in the second column start to add the tasks involved in each stage, adding a new row to the spreadsheet for each additional one (you can, of course, add more tasks at a later point in the same way).

Now include a column with your estimate for 'total hours required' on each of the subtasks, and a second column for 'total hours completed'. It is easy to set up a third column which will automatically subtract these numbers, showing how many hours you still need to spend on each task. It will be motivating to see these numbers reduce. If any task is estimated to take over 10 hours, it would be a good idea to subdivide it (perhaps just into 'part 1', 'part 2' etc).

Another useful feature is to include deadlines of when you need (or aim) to get tasks done by; it's then possible to reorder the spreadsheet so that it lists the rows in order of when they need to be done, should you choose to do so.

There is a natural tendency to underestimate planning time, so ensure that you have some leeway and contingency time in your plan, and set the spreadsheet or software up such that it is easy to edit on an ongoing basis.

Concluding comments

As can be seen, there are many considerations to take on board when producing good quality research, but no reason to think that such research won't be of wider interest and importance because you are a teacher or because the research is in a school. Designing a good research study is challenging, but in many ways it is the natural next step after you start to integrate research insights into your teaching practice, and evaluate their impact.

The key idea throughout this part of the book is that you CAN do this. Research is already part of your identity; becoming a researcher as well as a teacher can become part of your identity too. And as a teacher-researcher, you can be a creator—not just a consumer—of educational research.

Further reading

The next few chapters will guide you through the process of ethical research, controlling variables, and the most popular research methods. As with so much else in education, successful research is not so much a matter of ability but of knowledge and experience. If you have some background in conducting research on people (having done data gathering on a social science project as part of your undergraduate degree, for example, or through a practitioner enquiry project during your teacher preparation process) then this should be sufficient to direct you towards the key issues.

If, however, the idea of conducting any type of research on people is entirely new to you, you may wish to first consult a basic introduction to research which covers issues such as variables, hypotheses, ethics, control groups, and so forth.

Discussion questions

- Can teachers be researchers? And if so, should we use the term 'research', rather than 'action research' or 'practitioner enquiry'?
- What are the key differences between a proper research study and the kind of ongoing research-informed practice described earlier in this book?
- What is the difference between a pilot study and a full research study?
- Would you be willing and able to share the outcome of your research project?

Notes

1 It's worth noting two slightly different terms that are used about realism. 'Ecological validity' relates to the setting—is the study done in a place where participants normally spend time. School-based studies therefore all tend to

have high ecological validity. 'Mundane realism' is the extent to which research tasks are realistic. Even a study in your own classroom could lack mundane realism if you give learners a task which is not typically done in schools.

2 In addition, it's not just a matter of supporting or not supporting the theory, but also of finding out when it is useful and when it is not. A concept such as the spacing effect could be useful with some classroom tasks and not others. These limitations of an applied concept are known as 'boundary conditions', and it's very useful to learn about them.

3 Locke, E. A., and Latham, G. P. (2002). Building a practically useful theory of goal setting and task motivation: A 35-year odyssey. *American Psychologist*, 57(9), 705–717.

4 Latham, G. P., and Locke, E. A. (1991). Self-regulation through goal setting. *Organizational Behavior and Human Decision Processes*, 50(2), 212–247.

5 Sagor, R. (2000). *Guiding school improvement with action research*. Alexandria, Virginia: ASCD.

Conducting ethical research

All researchers have a responsibility to ensure that their research participants and other people involved in the research are treated ethically, and teacher-researchers are no exception to this rule. Perhaps the most important lesson of this book is that schools and teacher-researchers should maintain ethical standards that are every bit as high as those used by university-based researchers.

However, the processes and structures involved are different. A university-based researcher may need to first apply for approval from their institutional ethics board, and having obtained that, then apply to a local authority or academy chain who would then give (or refuse) permission to conduct research in their schools. Only at that point with they be able to ask individual schools and teachers to take part.

The teacher-researcher is in a slightly different position—they are both the person conducting the research and an employee of the school or organisation who has pastoral responsibility for the participants, i.e. the pupils. This does not have to make the research awkward or harder to do, but does require an awareness of essential ethical standards, and engaging with or establishing a process that will allow these standards to be applied effectively and in a way that is free from bias. This chapter guides you through the process of ensuring that your research is ethical.

Do I need to think about research ethics?

There are certain areas where a teacher does not need to worry about research ethics, simply because this issue is already covered by the existing standards of professionalism. For example, there are no ethical concerns with trying to do something which you think will lead to learning, or benefit your pupils in some other way. After all, you don't need to be a teacher-researcher to try out new tasks, techniques, or to make changes in response to professional reading or perceived learner needs.

Where do the ethical issues lie then? There are three main areas:

- If you are planning to use the information that you gather on pupils (e.g. grades, behaviour records) for something other than an educational purpose—such as for publication.
- If you plan to do something which is of uncertain benefit, and to evaluate it in a way that will involve trying it out on some pupils and not others.
- If you plan to test something which you are fairly certain will be useful to the learners, and wish to use another group of learners as a control group.

In all of the above cases, you are potentially doing something (or not doing something) to pupils or with their personal data that might not be in their best interests. This doesn't make it impossible to do, but there needs to be a process to ensure that any harm is both minimised and well-justified.

An ethical code of conduct

The main body which oversees educational research in the UK is the British Educational Research Association (BERA), and they provide a **code of conduct** for all educational researchers in any setting. It is essential that you are aware of their guidelines, interpreting them as they were intended and following them not just in letter but in spirit. The British Psychological Society (BPS) also provides guidelines which are highly relevant to a lot of primary research into human behaviour, including areas such as learning, memory and identity.

Key principles

Most of the key ethical principles are quite similar across different codes. The most important elements are as follows:

- Participants must not be endangered, harmed or distressed by any aspect of the investigation. Distress could include anything that embarrasses or humiliates participants or causes them a level of worry, stress or anxiety beyond what might occur in an everyday classroom situation. Colleagues and research partners should likewise not be endangered, harmed or distressed.

- Participants should give **informed consent** to take part in the study. By 'informed', this means that they know what they are consenting to, including the fact that the activity will be part of a research project, what it's about, how long it will take, and what will be done with their data. If participants are schoolchildren below the age of 16, they are too young to give consent independently, and therefore parental consent should be obtained in addition to the child expressing a willingness to take part (as noted above, you don't need to get consent if what you will be doing is simply trying to improve your teaching in some way).

- Participants have a right to withdraw from the study at any time (if the experiment has been completed, they can still withdraw their data). They should be informed of this at the outset.

- Participants should not be deceived unless there is no possible alternative— and if any information is kept from them, then they should be filled in at the earliest opportunity. Acceptable forms of deception might include keeping the precise aims of the study from participants prior to data gathering, if it was felt that sharing this information would put participants under pressure to act in a particular way, or otherwise bias the results. Unacceptable forms of deception could include lying about the nature of the study, such as pretending your research is about study skills when it is actually a study of peer pressure.

- Participant data should be kept secure. Analysis should be done anonymously, but it must be possible for the research team to identify participants' data in case they choose to withdraw—this is typically done by giving them a unique number or code. Any publications based on participant data should be anonymous and it must not be possible to otherwise identify individuals. Overall, data should be kept in accordance with data protection laws, and should be destroyed once no longer required for the research.

Case study: the ethics process

Clearly a key factor in making ethical decisions about school-based research is to have a background in research methodology and an awareness of standard ethical guidelines. But is that enough? Consider the case below:

> Arnold is the headteacher of a small secondary school in north Wales. A keen advocate of evidence-based practice, he feels that there is a strong argument for teachers getting to grips with educational research by conducting their own research projects.
>
> As he has a PhD in education and has previously studied moral philosophy, Arnold feels that he has good knowledge of research ethics. He therefore asked all staff to submit research proposals directly to him. At the first assembly of the year, he announced that everyone is expected to submit at least one proposal over the course of the academic year, unless they already have a current project ongoing.

(continued)

(continued)

> When projects arrive in his inbox, Arnold reads them and provides feedback on whether the project can proceed as it is, or what changes are required.

In the case above, Arnold has considerable power and control as headteacher. This allows him to autonomously approve research projects, and his background makes it likely that he has sufficient knowledge to gauge the main ethical issues.

However, there are some difficulties with this model. Universities tend to have a board or panel, rather than a single person in charge of ethics. This allows a variety of perspectives and interests to get a voice, and minimises the likelihood that personal relationships will bias the process (Arnold approving the projects proposed by his friends, for example). No matter how well qualified he is, Arnold won't have engaged with every possible kind of research.

Secondly, there is an issue with the way he is using his administrative power. Firstly, teachers are being coerced into proposing projects that they may have no real desire to do. This is not the best way to build a research culture (though this is not unique to schools—university staff face similar pressures). At universities, ethics scrutiny is not carried out by departmental management, keeping contractual targets (such as an aim to publish one study per year) separate from the decision over whether a particular project is approved or not.

Arnold's enthusiasm for teacher research engagement is essentially very positive, but it may bias his judgement of what is in the pupils' best interests, especially for projects that involve gathering pupil data. It would be better to have several voices involved.

The practice of consent

As noted above, informed consent means that the participants agree to take part in the study in full knowledge of what is going to happen.

Consent should also be obtained in a way that is not subject to coercion. This is actually quite difficult for a staff member to achieve, at least for research into their own pupils—as you have power over them, can you be sure that their consent is really freely given? And if they do agree, could it just be because everyone else in class is agreeing, and they don't want to feel left out? One way to avoid this issue is to present research tasks on an opt-in basis. You could run a task in class, and then ask them to submit a consent form to you if they are happy for their data to be used in your analysis.

Anyone who is not legally an adult can't consent to take part in research on their own behalf. Even a 14–15 year old, who may well understand the purpose and nature of the study, will be subject to parental consent, whereby a letter must be given to parents to consent on their behalf. It's important to remember that the pupil still needs to consent—so even if the parents have given the go ahead, a pupil could still pull out if the research makes them uncomfortable or distressed.

The situation with pupils aged 16+ is slightly trickier. On one level they are legally adults, able to make important decisions for themselves, but the school or local authority may still include them in a parental consent policy for research studies. Once they reach university level (which could be as young as age 16 or 17 for some) students would be expected to give consent to take part in research on their own behalf, and parents might not even know about it. It might be best to check with your management or local authority as to how they view the status of older pupils. A compromise might be to ask for older pupils' consent directly, but to insist on an information letter going to their parent or guardian as well.

How to avoid harm

'Harm' to participants or colleagues is quite a broad term—it could include a variety of things from minor physical dangers to psychological trauma. In the real world, it is impossible to be absolutely certain that participants will not come to any harm during the research, but it is important to avoid research designs where participants could be placed in embarrassing situations. Be wary of designs which involve putting an unusual focus on particular learners, forcing them to take part in learning activities with which they might not be comfortable, or requiring them to speak out in a group of strangers (as could be the case with a focus group—see Chapter 12).

From the research

Key issue: what is stress, and how do we minimise it?

What the research says: **stress** is a bodily reaction to events that exceed a person's ability to cope. The events that cause stress, sometimes referred to as stressors, can have a cumulative effect, but the person's psychological interpretation of events and their preferences also play a key role.[1] For example, background music that helps one person to focus may be stressful to another, and even no stimulus at all—being asked to sit in silence—can be stressful to some. Researchers have noticed that in terms of health, it is often the small, day-to-day stressors that have the biggest effect on health, rather than major events.[2]

Our surroundings, education and social interactions can all cause stress, but this is not always a bad thing. Researcher Hans Selye noted that stress can have either a positive or negative effect.[3] A certain amount of pressure can be stimulating, such as the effect of a bit of friendly competition.

One issue that makes people react less well to pressure is the feeling that events are outside of their control. This means that if people feel that negative events are happening to them and there is nothing they can do about it, stress will increase. In contrast, feeling in control of pleasant or unpleasant outcomes can reduce stress. Researchers call this having an 'internal locus of control'.[4] Allowing participants a choice of whether and when to take part in research, then, is not only more ethical in terms of respecting their rights, but is also likely to reduce harm in the form of stress.

Setting up an ethics process

It is important that any research practices take account of ethical consid-erations from the start. Many of the guidelines may seem like common sense (perhaps you could make the correct choices yourself without any help!), but it is an important and well-established standard that your research plan is scrutinised by an impartial group of professionals before the research commences. This means that you have to convince some-one outside of the research project itself that enough steps are being taken to avoid any ethical flaws or breaches.

It may be that you are conducting a research project in collaboration with a university or as part of a course such as a Masters in Education or PhD—if so, it will be simple (and probably mandatory) for you to submit your research proposal to the university's **ethical review board**. These boards meet regularly, but you should allow plenty of time and a certain amount of flexibility in your planned timings to allow for the possibility that they may ask for more information or for modifications to your ideas.

What if you are conducting research within a school with no external partner? One way to tackle this is to seek out a partner research organi-sation who will give you feedback on your plan. Another possibility is to find a way of initiating an ethics approval process in your own context. This could mean establishing an ethical review board within the school itself, or among a local cluster of schools, local authority, academy chain or so on. While this may seem a daunting prospect, any organisation which promotes research among its teachers should have some kind of ethics process in place, and if they do not already scrutinise research that is being done on pupils whose welfare is their responsibility, it is certainly worth suggesting that they begin to do so! In the long run, an in-house ethics board may be a quicker and cheaper approach than relying on a third party.

It may be that as the research-active teacher who raises this issue, the school asks you to initiate a suitable ethics process (or perhaps you are already responsible for research within the school). If you find yourself in this situation, a key principle is to ensure that a similar standard of ethical scrutiny is taking place as would be the case in a university set-ting (or better). Principles to consider could include:

- Setting out a structure and procedures in writing, stating things like the number of people on the board and the frequency of meetings.
- Usually a board has a chair—how will this person be chosen, and will it be a rotating appointment?
- Will there be at least one person on the board who is external to the organisation? A university academic may be willing to play this role.

Besides the points above, there are some things to think about when inviting colleagues to sit on the ethics board:

- The experience of potential members—have any sat on an ethics board before, or submitted their own ethics application? Members who have conducted a Masters or PhD which involved research on people, even if it was not directly educational, will have a better insight into the process.
- Are the board members going to be impartial? For example, if the school has an active group of four or five teachers who are conducting most of the in-house research, it would be best if the same teachers didn't constitute the school's ethics board.
- Will there be any conflicts of interest? Consider whether there might be a personal or professional conflict that could affect the decision making process. For example, a potential board member who is trying to promote a research agenda may be biased towards approving projects, while others may be on close personal terms with the most active teacher-researchers.
- Are there people with child protection experience on the board?

Although the main purpose of an organisation's ethical review board may be to review proposed new practitioner research projects, it may also find itself playing another important function—managing external requests for research access to the school or cluster. Independent schools, academy chains and local authorities receive many such requests. Again having an in-house board is a logical step, and one which is likely to better protect pupils' interests than having these decisions being carried out by a single person (as in the case study on p. 115).

Feedback on projects

With an ethics process in place, there is of course a need to feed back on colleagues' research proposals. Inevitably, this will involve rejecting some proposals on ethical or practical grounds.

Researchers are most commonly asked to make changes to their proposals rather than being flatly rejected. Some simple examples include:

- Requesting further information or clarification.
- Requesting edits to any errors or inconsistencies.
- Asking for a risk assessment for some aspect of the task.
- Suggesting a change to the plan for data analysis or management, e.g. to ensure security of data.
- Asking the researcher to consider offering more of a benefit to participants, such as free study advice to any pupil who takes part in a memory experiment.

In some cases, though, more complex changes may be required, and a meeting between the board and the teacher-researcher can be helpful. In this forum, changes to the methodology can be agreed. For example, could the same aims be achieved in a shorter period of time? Could the task be less invasive?

Overall, the research should be minimally harmful for maximum benefit. Even a fairly innocuous task may be rejected if there is no clear benefit to carrying out the project. As a researcher submitting a proposal, then, it is important to give a rationale for why the work needs to be carried out.

Research project: as noted, it is essential to obtain informed consent from participants, and to find ways of storing their data securely and in a way that allows them to later withdraw from the research if necessary. This project focuses on putting these procedures in place.

(continued)

121

(continued)

How to do it: firstly, a research study should use a participant information sheet (or page on a screen) to inform participants about the study. Among other things it should say who is doing the research, why they are doing it, what the task will involve, and how long it will take. It usually includes the aim and title of the study, too.

Next, draw up a consent form. Having already briefed the participants with task-specific information, this can be kept fairly simple, but it should inform participants of their rights. For example, it should let them know that the research is not mandatory, that they have a right to withdraw at any point, and how long their data will be held for. It should also tell them that any analysis and publication will be anonymous. Finally there should be a space for them to sign and date the form. Have a look at examples online as you prepare your own version.

Both the consent form and participant information sheet can be created in template form, to allow other teacher-researchers to adapt them to their needs.

You should also figure out a procedure that will allow you to later find out who each response belongs to (e.g. if they want to withdraw), for example by putting the same unique code onto both consent form and a task response sheet or questionnaire.

Lastly, you should work on data storage. Again, this could be a written school-wide policy if you have overall responsibility for research. Research data and backups should be kept securely, with password protection. If you have no idea how to do this, speak to a relevant colleague who does—every school is already dealing with sensitive personal information, so the expertise is available to you.

Concluding comments

As discussed, research projects should be minimally harmful for maximum benefit. While it is not incumbent on classroom teachers to seek ethical permissions before they make improvements to their teaching practice or gather 'data' in the form of feedback, there should be careful consideration given to any proposals which go beyond that, including any analysis or publication of learner data outside of normal educational practices.

As discussed, your employer may choose to set up an ethics board or equivalent process, and there can be an opportunity for you as a teacher-researcher to engage with this and begin to guide the research of others. This establishes you as a role model and potentially as a mentor; Chapter 15 explores the building of a culture of research, perhaps culminating in a school 'research centre'.

Although meeting ethical standards may seem arduous, a lot of the requirements fit with existing teacher professional standards about treating learners with respect, keeping their data confidential, and working in the best interests of their learning and well-being. Indeed, most ethical research practices become habits after a short time—but it is always helpful to seek objective feedback on your plans.

Further reading

There are numerous codes of ethics aimed at researchers, but the BERA guide to ethics is the best place for education researchers to start (this can be accessed at www.bera.ac.uk).

In addition, any textbook on conducting classroom-based research projects, e.g. as part of Masters' level study, will have guidance on ethics.

Discussion questions

- Would it be ethical to try out a task on your learners if you have good reason to think that it is based on flawed theories of learning?
- Is it ok to ask one group of learners to sit quietly and read during a classroom task, so that they can form a control group?

● A colleague plans to keep their class of Year 7s back for 30 minutes at the end of the school day to complete a research survey. What should they do or consider in advance?

Notes

1 Lazarus, R. S., and Folkman, S. (1987). Transactional theory and research on emotions and coping. *European Journal of Personality*, 1(3), 141–169.
2 DeLongis, A., Coyne, J. C., Dakof, G., Folkman, S., and Lazarus, R. S. (1982). Relationship of daily hassles, uplifts, and major life events to health status. *Health Psychology*, 1(2), 119–136.
3 Selye, H. (1956). *The stress of life*. New York: McGraw-Hill.
4 Kormanik, M. B., and Rocco, T. S. (2009). Internal versus external control of reinforcement: A review of the locus of control construct. *Human Resource Development Review*, 8(4), 463–483.

Controlling research variables

In the complex environment of a classroom, how do you know that an effect—such as improved learning or behaviour—happened for the reasons you assume? For teachers who have little or no background in educational research, this can be confusing. And of course, we want to avoid errors in our conclusions.

As we have seen, there are many things that can affect the data that we gather in research projects, and certain sources of bias. When planning a classroom-based research project, it is important that these are accounted for in some way. It's not always possible to have complete certainty as to why findings have turned out a particular way, but we need to at least minimise the effect of unwanted outside variables, and to provide a rationale as to why other influences on learners' behaviour probably did not account for any changes that we observed. This chapter guides you through this aspect of the research design process.

Parts of this chapter are necessarily quite technical, but there is a good reason for this; they will help you not only with planning and carrying out better research, but also with understanding and critiquing other research that you read. The chapter mainly focuses on gathering primary (i.e. new) data; use of existing data is the focus of the next chapter.

Data and variables in your research

Two issues that play a role in any practical research study are variables and data:

- Anything that we measure or record in research—pupil behaviour, test scores, answers to a question and so on—forms our *data*, that is, the numbers and descriptions that we actually gather for later analysis.

- These data may tell us something about at least one **variable** (or possibly more than one). A variable is anything that can change in a particular person, such as their level of knowledge, their mood, their competence at a task and so on.

As might be obvious, there can be more than one way of measuring a particular variable. If you want to measure a variable that you label 'pupil motivation', you could do so by recording data on their body language, or asking them questions such as 'do you enjoy this subject'. In the case of a questionnaire, many different questions could be attempting to measure the same variable.

To put it another way, data is what we gather in the form of measurements, numbers and verbal records, while a variable is a theoretical construct that guides data gathering and helps us to make sense of the data.

Some variables—such as a person's height or age—are fairly easy to measure. However, in education, variables are often quite hard to measure, and not necessarily obvious on the surface. What data would you gather in order to find out about a pupil's creativity, their locus of control, their resilience or their mindset? These things have to be measured indirectly, through a well-chosen task. Even measuring something like their ability in a maths is not totally straightforward—different tests would give different results.

It follows that a set of data and a variable are not the same thing. A classic example is a score on an IQ test (data), which does not necessarily indicate the variable that the test is designed to measure (i.e. intelligence) in a satisfactory way. Indeed, because variables often rest on theories which are open to debate, some might argue that certain variables (such as intelligence) do not even exist, and that any data recorded (such as one pupil scoring higher on an IQ test than another pupil does) indicates *something else*—a different variable, such as motivation or *practice*.

Research variables and hypotheses

Variables are not something that we only think about after gathering data, when we begin our analysis. On the contrary, the entire research study is typically designed because we have a theory-based idea about how one variable affects another, and we want to gather and analyse data in order to find out more about this.

If you look back to the aims and particularly to the specific research questions discussed in the earlier chapters, these tended to express a relationship between variables. For example, perhaps your research question asked whether pupils behave better when working in pairs than they do when working in groups. In this case, the two key research variables would be:

  Pupil grouping (pairs or groups)

  and

  Pupil behaviour

In this example, the research hypothesises a cause-and-effect relationship: one variable is thought to affect the other. The study would then aim to gather data to shed light on this hypothesis—to determine whether the research hypothesis (i.e. prediction—see below) is correct or not.

Typically, these research variables are called the **independent variable (IV)** (the one which is thought to cause a change in the other—pupil grouping, in the last example), and the **dependent variable (DV)** (the variable that is thought to change as a result of changes in the independent variable). Collectively, they may sometimes be called the 'research variables':

Research variables

  Independent variable/IV: pupil grouping (pairs or groups)
  Dependent variable/DV: pupil behaviour

These terms will already be familiar to most science and social science teachers. It's not entirely necessary to use the standard terminology just to conduct (or even write up) a study, but you may come across them in other contexts or find it useful to clarify these variables using standard terminology when talking to co-researchers.

Experiments

Usually, educational researchers don't study just one pupil—they take multiple measurements, perhaps from a whole class, or from several. This can allow them to compare the class under different conditions.

In an experiment, the term **condition** means a particular level or value of the independent variable that is being studied. Following from the last example, a researcher could compare pupil behaviour under two conditions—one where they are seated in groups, and another where they are seated in pairs. The two or more values or levels of the IV (in this example, pairs versus groups) lead to two or more conditions. An experiment doesn't need to take place in a lab; the term refers to the logic of what is done (looking for a cause-and-effect relationship between variables) rather than to the context.

A similar logic is at play in a **randomised controlled trial (RCT)**— a particular type of experiment that uses a control group, and which randomly allocates some participants (or classes or schools) to a control condition, and others to one or more experimental conditions.

It's unlikely that a RCT will be the starting point for most teacher research projects, given the scale (they generally involve several schools) and funding involved. They have also been criticised on the basis that it is difficult to maintain the fidelity of the intervention (that is, the teachers in the school might not stick to it) and due to the ethical complaint of some schools being used as a control group. Nevertheless, it is worth keeping an open mind on this as a possibility for the future, especially if you go on to establish a research network (see Chapter 16) that involves other local schools and/or universities.

Even if you are not running a RCT, you should still consider whether you can randomise how participants are allocated to conditions in your research, as doing so will reduce bias in your results. If participants are going to take part in more than one condition (such as the two seating arrangements described above), you could randomly decide which arrangement they experience first.

From the research

<u>Key issue</u>: how easily biased are research measurements? As we start to gather research data in a more systematic way, it's important to think about the various ways in which the data that we gather could be distorted.

<u>What the research says</u>: the very nature of gathering data brings with it certain biases. Unfortunately, the presence of the researcher herself or himself can cause bias! Just as you may behave differently when your boss is in the room, research participants are affected by the presence of the person who is running a study. This is known as the **researcher effect**. It's worth asking, would the findings be the same if the task/ observation was administered by another teacher or by a student? Could your enthusiasm or personal relationship with the learners be affecting the results? That's not always a bad thing (it's natural that they would behave differently with a teacher that they know and trust compared to with a stranger), but it can affect the extent to which your findings will generalise to other contexts.

A second factor to be aware of is that the learner themselves may behave unnaturally just because they know they are being measured, regardless of who administers a task. This could take various forms. One, often termed the **good participant effect**, is where research participants try their best on a task in order to please the researcher or just because they view this as the norms of the social situation.[1] This may lead to distorted findings, for example with pupils doing much better on a research task

(continued)

(continued)

than would be the case if it were an ordinary school activity. An opposite (but equally unhelpful) process is the **screw-you effect**, where participants make no effort on the task because they know it's of no benefit to them, or they simply wish to undermine the process. This might happen if pupils are kept back after a class to do a task, knowing that it has no relevance to their courses and grades.

Researchers themselves may be biased in their allocation of a task or in their scoring of data. According to social psychologist Rob Rosenthal, people are often unconsciously biased in their judgements simply due to their expectations. In his research, he found that observers watching lab rats which had been labelled as 'bright' rats judged their maze-running behaviour as more successful and 'dull' rats less so, even though these labels had actually been allocated at random.[2] Shockingly, a similar finding was found in a follow-up study of schoolchildren, with those labelled as high IQ (but actually chosen randomly) treated differently in a way that led to them actually doing better on a later IQ test.[3] This links closely to the idea of confirmation bias, discussed in Chapter 4.

We can't entirely avoid these problems, but research studies can be designed in such a way as to minimise their effects. One approach is to operate a **double blind design**, where neither the researcher nor the participant knows which condition of a study the participant has been allocated to. That is, they don't know if a group has been predicted to do better or to do worse (although participants may be able to easily work this out if they do both conditions, such as trying a task with and without background noise!). Bias in judgements can also be partly accounted for by scoring tasks in an anonymised way, and by recruiting a colleague as a second, impartial scorer.

There are also biases inherent in many questionnaires—these are discussed in Chapter 11.

Confounding variables

In any research, from primary school science projects to academic publications, there is a fundamental issue that must be observed: we can't determine whether one variable affects another unless we keep all other variables controlled. This is a universal part of the scientific method; sometimes in school science it is referred to as running a 'fair test'.

For example, if you want to know whether a particular type of plant food 'brand A' works better than a rival 'brand B', you can experiment by trying each of them out, but you'd need to keep all other variables that affect plant growth (light, temperature, type of soil, etc) the same in both cases.

We would also need to test it multiple times on different plants, to rule out the possibility that one of the plants was hardier and grew more vigorously for reasons unrelated to the plant food. Therefore there would be a 'brand A condition' and a 'brand B condition', each with multiple plants being measured, and an average outcome calculated.

If a variable is not kept constant, and instead affects one condition of the experiment more than the other, then it is known as a **confounding variable** (or 'confound'). In the plant example, perhaps the plants that we feed with brand A are also kept closer to the window in our lab. This would lead to a confounding variable—if these plants

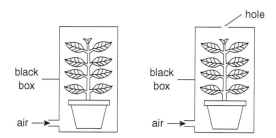

Figure 9.1 If an experiment aimed to test the effect of nutrients on plant growth, all other variables – for example light – would have to be kept constant.

grow better, we don't know if this is due to the food, or due to differences in lighting or temperature. The data become impossible to interpret, because we can't separate one possible cause of the change from another.

In education, there are often multiple variables affecting anything that we measure. We might give a child a spelling test, for example, but this is not just affected by a variable that we might term their 'spelling competence'. There are many other things that could affect the test score, including the child's anxiety, how recently they practised the words on the test, whether they got a good night's sleep last night, and so on. How do we account for the inherent messiness of variables in education?

If the spelling test was part of an experiment where we are investigating spaced practice, we would want to ensure that the two groups that we compared and the way that they were treated were <u>alike in every way except for the IV</u>. This means keeping other variables constant ('controlling' these variables). Some issues to consider in such a classroom study are:

- Pre-existing difference in attainment: consider choice of participants in the conditions that are being compared, ensuring that they are comparable or matched in some way. This is discussed further below (see 'Research groupings' on p. 139).

- Task time: all groups of learners must have the same amount of time to do a research task.

- Giving identical instructions: this is best done using scripted, standardised instructions, especially when more than one researcher is gathering the data.

Overall, we need to be as systematic as possible, and to consider and rule out any possible confounds, some of which will be specific to the task. For the most part, this is done via thorough planning, and avoiding the biases discussed in the box above (see From the research on p. 129).

Interactions

While it is often undesirable for other variables to interfere with a simple cause-and-effect relationship between an IV and DV that are under investigation, in other cases it might be the aim of the research! Let's imagine that we are investigating the expertise reversal effect (see Chapter 13), a part of cognitive load theory which suggests that experts benefit from simpler instructions. As part of a study, we may investigate the role of giving simple or detailed instructions on how easily and quickly learners complete the task:

Research variables

- IV: instructions (simple or complex)
- DV: time taken for pupil to complete task

In a simple study, we might expect a simple cause-and-effect relationship. However, part of the theory states that detailed instructions will be helpful for beginners, but a distraction (extraneous cognitive load) for more advanced learners. Therefore there is an additional IV, learner expertise:

Research variables

- IV: instructions (simple or complex)
- IV: learner expertise (beginner or advanced)
- DV: time taken for pupil to complete task

When analysing, we are expecting to see an **interaction**—that is, we expect one IV to affect the other. This is often displayed on a line graph, as shown below:

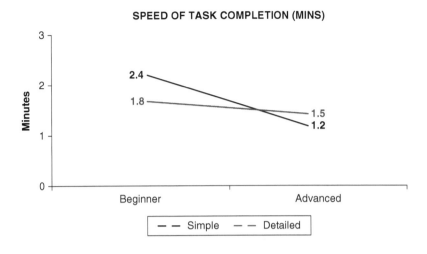

SPEED OF TASK COMPLETION (MINS)

While it's not necessary to include more than one IV in your study, these interactions are often among the most important findings in educational research. They help us to understand that it's not always a case of 'x works', and more a case of 'x is helpful in certain situations, and unhelpful in others'.

Alternative and null hypotheses

Two other pieces of terminology that you may come across as you engage more fully with research are the terms for different types of hypotheses. Firstly, the researcher can state a null hypothesis—a prediction that the IV will not affect the DV, and any difference between conditions is due to chance factors.

Again, you don't necessarily need to use this terminology; the hypothesis is typically not labelled as such in the research write-up, but it can be useful to help you clarify your thinking and express a prediction and rationale objectively.

The null hypothesis states some kind of a baseline assumption—it is what can be assumed if the effect or interaction we are investigating does not occur. It could be based on prior, well-established research findings or a theory that is widely accepted.

Next the researcher makes a prediction of what will happen if the IV does affect the DV. This is often termed an alternative (or 'experimental') hypothesis, and it is expressed in terms of the specific task under investigation.

The following example expresses both a null and alternative hypothesis in a single paragraph:

> *Previous studies have established that multitasking, such as by doing an organisation task at the same time as taking a phone call, can hinder performance. However, it is unclear whether this will vary depending on the sex of the individual. If there is no such sex difference, it can be assumed that multitasking will impact the performance of males and females to a similar extent in comparison to their baseline scores on either task separately. However, if it is the case that women can multitask more successfully, then women will show smaller reductions in their task performances compared to men.*

This kind of paragraph (which might be specified in even more detail if the precise kind of task under investigation had been explored in the literature review) tends to come at the end of the introduction section of a published paper, acting as a hinge point between that section and the methodology section.

Case study: Mr Dexter

In the following case, a teacher tries to implement an educational theory that he is aware of and enthusiastic about. As you read it, consider what forms of data Mr Dexter gathers, and what variables he fails to control:

> Mr Dexter is conducting a classroom-based project on strategies for improving pupils' spelling in the primary school. Inspired by the concept of multiple intelligences, he decides

(continued)

(continued)

to set up several spelling activities for the pupils to work through, each based on a different form of intelligence from the theory (visual-spatial, linguistic, interpersonal, musical, bodily-kinaesthetic, etc). Each activity is set up at a small cluster of tables in the classroom in a carousel format. Every pupil is given a spelling test before the activities, and then another spelling test after completing all of the activities. Mr Dexter also asks pupils to fill out a short questionnaire, which asks how much they enjoyed the spelling activities.

Looking at the data, Mr Dexter sees that on average, pupils did better on the spelling test after the activities than they had done before. He also finds that they liked the musical and bodily-kinaesthetic activities best, and so he resolves to use those more.

A positive of this case is that Mr Dexter is making an attempt to engage with the research, and also that he used a pre-test and post-test comparison. However, there are a number of flaws that make his findings difficult to interpret. One notable flaw is that there is no control group. This means that it is hard to know how much of the improvement on the second test is simply due to practice on the tests themselves, and how much (if any) is due to the classroom activities. You would expect people to do better at a second attempt at a test, even without further practice!

Secondly, Mr Dexter is relying heavily on self-reported enjoyment of tasks. While pupil enjoyment of schoolwork is certainly important, it isn't a reliable proxy for learning. Just because the pupils enjoyed the musical task more, doesn't mean that it improved their spelling more than the other activities.

There are other flaws, such as the lack of control in a carousel task—the learners may spend much more time on one task than another, or may be distracted by others at the same station. This can be acceptable for classroom practice, but is not ideal for a research task.

Extraneous variables

As can be seen from the case study of Mr Dexter, a major flaw with any study is allowing outside variables to affect the findings. A well-designed study will keep other such variables to a minimum.

As noted earlier, your research design must avoid confounding variables. However, even if such flaws are avoided, there will be some variables that cause random error in results. Perhaps one pupil scores badly on a task because they are especially tired. Perhaps one pupil happens to be better at the task than his or her peers. It's impossible to fully avoid such variables causing some 'noise' in your findings. These are known as **extraneous variables**.

Extraneous variables include minor background noise, variations between participants (differences such as ability and motivation), and low-level differences in available time such as the fact that if a task sheet is handed out to a group, some people will get their sheets earlier than others.

The effects of such extraneous variables should be minimised as far as possible. This can include conducting the study in a quiet room at the end of the school day. If this happens, then as long as these variables don't affect one group more than another in our comparison, they are are an acceptable and inevitable part of research, especially field research.

However, it may occasionally happen that an extraneous variable affects one group more than another. In the groups versus pairs study discussed earlier, perhaps a lot of noise from building work outside begins just as the class start to try the task in groups, after having previously done the paired task in silence. If we then find that the pupils behave better on the pairs task, this becomes hard to interpret—was it because of the grouping, or because the noisy conditions distracted them? In this case, something that is usually considered an acceptable extraneous variable (background noise) could become a confounding variable, as it could skew the results.

Comparing groups

The case study also noted that a control group would make it easier to interpret the results from Mr Dexter's intervention in pupils' spelling.

The most obvious ways to do this are to divide the class so that some are exposed to the intervention and others are not.

However, this causes a dilemma—unlike in a laboratory psychology experiment, where it's acceptable to have a control group, your role as teacher is first and foremost to help all of your learners. Anything that we want to test because we have good reason to believe it will improve learning should, arguably, be offered to all. For that reason, having a control group is not always a viable or ethical option.

There are several ways to tackle this dilemma:

- In the case of a new intervention with uncertain benefits, we may wish to start this on a very small scale, such as in a single lesson. This could be trialled with very little impact on either the learners who try it or those who don't, either positive or negative. If it looks promising, it could then be expanded.

- An intervention could be offered as a voluntary choice. For example, pupils could be offered the option of trying a new way of revising spelling words in their homework. However, interpreting this can be difficult—perhaps the more motivated and high-attaining pupils will choose to try the new method, leading to a confounding variable.

- Two halves of the class (or two similar classes) could be used, but both could be offered the intervention at different times. For example, you could try your intervention in week one, and then the comparison tasks in week two. This way, both groups get the chance of the new evidence-based intervention, as well as a class which is more 'business as usual' for comparison.

- Historical data can be used. For example, if you have data on how your A-Level classes performed in a mock exam last year, you could trial an intervention with the current year's class, and then give them the same exam. In effect, the previous year's pupils are acting as a control group, but there is no ethical dilemma because they were taught according to your best efforts and knowledge at the time.

⦿ You could offer the intervention to all of your learners, and compare them to other classes taught by your colleagues.

All of these options are useful, but each comes with its own practical issues and difficulties with interpreting the results. For example, if two classes are compared, are they actually equivalent in ability? Often class groupings are done non-randomly. Even groupings that are alphabetic by surname or based on feeder areas/primary schools could lead to bias in results. If comparing this year's class to historical data, can you be sure that this year's class aren't generally better or worse in some way? Also, other variables might have changed over the past year—you might be teaching better this time round, or some outside factor in the school (such as the prevailing attitudes to work and revision) may have changed.

Therefore it can be said that none of the options are perfect, but each offers a potential way of comparing two conditions, provided that sufficient thought is given to confounding variables. Similar issues arise if the research involves comparing groups of teachers rather than pupils.

Research groupings

The issue of control groups brings up the broader design issues of how research participants are allocated to groups. There are two main ways of doing this:

⦿ The same participants do both/all research conditions.

⦿ A separate group of participants takes part in each condition.

Testing the same participants more than once leads to a further consideration: if they do better in the second condition, is this simply because they got better with practice? For this reason you may decide to split them into sub-groups, one of which does the intervention first, and one of which does it second.

In some cases it would be impractical or impossible for participants to do both versions of an intervention (such as doing the same task in groups *and* in pairs), but it is best if possible to test the same people on both conditions—after all, you are then comparing like with like (participant ability is not going to be a confounding variable). This could be achieved by using very similar materials for the two conditions. In the earlier example, the pupils could do one task in pairs, and then a very similar task in groups.

Research project: now that we have investigated research ethics and design, why not try the example discussed above—what difference to behaviour does it make (if any) if learners are seated in different arrangements? Or alternatively, you could measure a DV other than behaviour, such as speed of completing school work.

How to do it: Once ethical permission has been obtained and you have thought about how the data will be used, in essence, this is as simple as moving your classroom around so that pupils are seated in pairs for one task, and in groups for another. This could be done simultaneously; if, for example, you have 24 pupils, you could set up three clusters of four, as well as six pairs of desks.

You then need to decide upon tasks. Whatever the tasks are, they need to be reasonably matched in terms of difficulty and how engaging they are. Then, just as with any carrousel-type class, you can ask learners to switch around after a period of time, thus allowing you to observe them in different settings.

It may be useful to recruit observers, perhaps from among the pupils themselves (or older peers). Their job will be to sit at the back of the room and rate the pairs/groups on their behaviour, how hard they are working, or whatever it is you choose to measure. Additionally (or as well), you could ask the pupils themselves to reflect on how engaged and hard working they and their group mates were during each task by completing a short questionnaire.

Concluding comments

This chapter has looked at some of the key considerations that class-room research needs to consider in order to get an accurate, unbiased idea of how one variable affects another. It has addressed the difference between variables and data, and considered the cause-and-effect relationships which can be determined using experiments and RCTs.

There are a great many ways to measure variables. This chapter has focused on experimental-type designs, but has not really focused on how the data is gathered in the first place. The next few chapters will look at some of the main methods of gathering quantitative (numerical) and qualitative (verbal) data.

Further reading

Hugh Coolican's 'Research Methods and Statistics in Psychology' (2014, Psychology Press) covers the issue of control of variables very thoroughly, as well as many other issues that are applicable to experimental research in education. It's also engagingly written and accessible.

Discussion questions

- What variables might affect a learner's work rate?
- What problems are there with asking learners to reflect on how well they learned or behaved?
- If you were going to compare the effect of two alternative work-sheets on the same topic, how might you gather unbiased data to see which was more effective?
- Might experiments be an inappropriate research method to use when investigating certain educational issues?
- Do you think you could conduct or participate in a large-scale RCT, involving several schools?

Notes

1 Orne, M. T. (1962). On the social psychology of the psychological experiment: With particular reference to demand characteristics and their implications. *American Psychologist*, 17(11), 776.
2 Rosenthal, R., and Fode, K. L. (1963). The effect of experimenter bias on the performance of the albino rat. *Behavioral Science*, 8(3), 183–189.
3 Rosenthal, R., and Jacobson, L. (1966). Teachers' expectancies: Determinants of pupils' IQ gains. *Psychological Reports*, 19(1), 115–118.

Correlation studies

We have now looked at research ethics, and the principle of identifying and controlling research variables. But before we delve deeper into the main methods used for data gathering, it will be useful to consider **correlation** studies. These typically use existing data, meaning that there are fewer ethical worries associated with them (although confidentiality of participant data must always be considered), and the teacher-researcher doesn't need to tackle the technical issues associated with using questionnaires or observations.

Correlation is widely used in the social sciences. It is a way of comparing the levels of two variables, in order to get an idea of how they rise or fall together. It notoriously does not prove **causation** (that is, a cause-and-effect link between the two variables cannot be demonstrated, unlike in an experiment), but can provide useful evidence, and the basis for further investigation. For example, if a link is found, this could then suggest a hypothesis for a future experimental study.

As such, a correlation study can provide a useful bridge point between integrated, classroom-based data gathering and a larger-scale teacher research project. It is a mainstream form of study and could potentially be publishable.

When is correlation used?

As a method of analysis, correlation could be used with new ('primary') data—answers gained from a questionnaire, for example—or with existing ('secondary') data. This chapter will focus particularly on the latter, but when we come on to talking about questionnaire design (see Chapter 11), correlation will again be considered as a useful option for data analysis.[1]

How does correlation work?

Although sometimes referred to as a research method, correlation is perhaps best thought of as a statistical technique. It is used to find the relationship between two variables, referred to as **co-variables**.[2]

Firstly, the researcher who is carrying out a correlation study needs to obtain a set of data relating to each co-variable. For example:

Variable 1: pupils' attainment in a subject;

Variable 2: the number of books they read per year.

Variable 1: how happy pupils feel;

Variable 2: how frequently they use social media.

Variable 1: how much feedback the pupil is given by the teacher;

Variable 2: how motivated the pupil is.

As can be seen from the examples, correlation studies are all about comparing two variables to one another (or rather, comparing two sets of data which are assumed to represent the two variables—see previous chapter!).

They can be highly suggestive of a cause-and-effect relationship: surely if pupils who read more books get a better exam score, their better grade is because they read more books? However, it is important to consider other possibilities:

- Reverse causation: variable 2 could be causing a change in variable 1. For the first example, perhaps people who generally get better exam grades are more motivated to read, or have more time to do so because they are not busy with resits.

- A third variable causing both changes: some other factor could influence both of the variables under investigation. In the second example, perhaps people who have a larger number of friends are both happier and busier on social media (note: there is no way of knowing directly from the correlation data what a third variable might be—we can only speculate).

- The relationship is spurious/accidental: sometimes, two variables change in the same direction, but the changes are not related to each other. A historical example is that there is a negative correlation between IQ scores in Britain and the marriage rate (IQ scores have risen as the number of people getting married has fallen over recent decades), but these changes are not directly related to each other (that is, it is probably wrong to conclude that people are getting smarter, leading to their being more sceptical about marriage—but we can't be entirely sure).

- It may be the case that the data that we use to represent one variable fails to accurately capture that variable. In the third example, if we ask pupils to rate their motivation on a scale of 1–10, their response may reflect how they want to be seen by the teacher, rather than their true level of motivation.

From the research

Key issue: does it make any difference if pupils are socially skilled? It has been argued[3] that our 'emotional intelligence'—which could also be described as our competence at dealing with social interactions and managing our own emotions—matters more than traditional measures of intelligence. But does the research support this, and does it lead to more academic success?

What the research says: one way of attempting to measure emotional intelligence (EI) is to present people with emotion-based problems,[4] and their scores on these can then be compared with existing data, such as measures of attainment or behaviour, using a correlation analysis. Such research does appear positive—high EI is associated with fewer absences and expulsions,[5] and better academic performance at all stages of schooling.[6]

(continued)

(continued)

However, this is an area where correlations can be problematic. What does it actually mean if learners who score higher for EI are doing better at school? It seems unlikely to be a case of reverse causation—passing exams causing emotional intelligence to increase. However, this could happen indirectly, if better attainment reduces stress, and lower stress levels contributes to better people skills. It could also be the case that those of us with better academic skills and knowledge are better at solving the tasks on an EI test—treating them as problems to solve, without necessarily being better at responding to such situations in real life. In this case, the data gathered would not accurately reflect the assumed underlying variable (i.e. would not be a valid measure).

There could also be a third variable that affects both EI and attainment, for example having calmer and more supportive parents. Those who benefit from such parenting might do better on their exams (due to more reliable support) and also have role models about how to interact socially, leading to better EI scores.

Finally, it's worth considering that correlation is blind to whether the variable we are measuring actually makes any theoretical sense. Tests of EI certainly tell us something—but what? There could be several separate skills, traits and personality factors that affect how well we do on such tests,[7] and performance at emotional or self-regulation tasks may also vary over time, depending on mood or recent experience. Some people doubt whether EI exists at all. Correlation simply analyses the data—it's up to the researcher to make sense of the underlying theory.

Carrying out the correlational analysis

Correlational analysis requires you to find a numerical score for every participant on at least two variables.

These scores also need to be ranged along a scale from high to low, where increases reflect higher levels of the variable (or to put it another way, they need to be at least *ordinal data*).[8] This means that you can't assign arbitrary numbers such as 1, 2, 3 to particular behaviours (e.g. three types of study habits) and use this as the basis for the analysis, for example.

Participant scores on the co-variables can then be used for two things:

- A statistical test is used to calculate the **correlation co-efficient**—a number that tells us how strong the correlation is, and what direction it is in.

- The data can be shown on a graph called a **scattergram**.

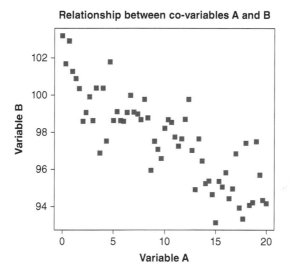

Relationship between co-variables A and B

The pattern of points on the scattergram gives an initial visual impression of the relationship between the co-variables:

- If high scores on one variable tend to go with high scores on the other and the points on the graph rise from left to right, there is a **positive correlation**. This shows us that high levels of one variable are associated with high levels of the other, and low levels with low—the two variables are somehow tied together. In the example from the scenario, this would mean that high EI scores are associated with high attainment (or behaviour) scores.

- If high scores on one variable tend to go with low scores in the other and the points on the graph fall from left to right there is a **negative correlation**. This shows a pattern like a see-saw—one rises as the other falls. In the example from the scenario, this would mean that high EI scores are associated with low attainment/behaviour scores.

To help researchers easily interpret the visual pattern on the graph, a line is drawn such that the distance between the points and the line is minimised. This is called the 'line of best fit'.

More precise information can be obtained using the correlation co-efficient. This expresses the strength of the relationship between the two co-variables on a scale ranging from −1 (a perfect negative correlation) through zero (no relationship at all) up to +1 (a perfect positive correlation).

Once you have all of the necessary data, a correlation co-efficient can be calculated using standard statistics software, or via an online tool (often this is as simple as typing in the scores from each variable into a website, and clicking 'calculate'). However there are different statistical tests with different technical assumptions, and if you don't have previous experience of this, it would be worthwhile to take advice from a statistician, mathematician or social scientist. The data need to be in pairs, so that for each participant you have one score for each co-variable.

What exactly the correlation co-efficient tells you depends on the study, but as a general rule, a co-efficient of between 0 and 0.3 (or -0.3) is considered weak, while anything above 0.7 (or -0.7) is considered strong. For some areas, such as the correlation between a particular variable and health outcomes, a weak correlation could still be important. Imagine you found a 0.2 correlation between how often people eat a particular food and their age of death, for example. This could be important, as part of the broader context of things that affect health and life expectancy. A similar argument could be made about academic attainment. However, again, it is worth emphasising that a correlation doesn't show that a variable—in this example, the food—is causing a change in the other variable—in this example, dying younger (it could be the case that people who are generally less healthy tend to eat more of this food, and the food itself makes no difference to health).

The stronger the relationship (either positive or negative), the closer points on the scattergram will be to the line of best fit. If there is no relationship at all (a zero correlation), the points will be scattered randomly, and it will be impossible to draw a line of best fit. This is not a bad finding, however, and can be very useful to establish.

Following up on a correlation

A strong correlation shows that two variables are consistently related, but, as noted above, cause and effect should not be assumed.

Let's imagine for a moment that you have analysed the relationship between a primary class's scores on a maths test and the number of books they have read (using data taken from class reading diaries). Without controlled experimentation, it is impossible to know which variable is affecting which. Could better literacy levels improve maths scores, perhaps because they are better at reading and analysing written scenario-based problems? Or have stronger maths skills made them more confident and motivated, boosting their reading? Could there be a third variable at play? We can't tell this from the data alone.

However, this doesn't mean that correlational analysis isn't useful. It's often the best way to begin to investigate an issue, raising vital questions and suggesting hypotheses for future studies. And correlational analysis can be conducted without any new data at all, making it potentially less arduous and ethically fraught for the new teacher-researcher.

Also, a strong correlation enables researchers to predict the value of one co-variable from the value of the other. Even if we don't know why maths outcomes and reading level correlate, we can predict that our most voracious readers will in general do better on maths tests than their peers. This could make it easier to target support where it is most needed. It might be unethical or impractical to achieve the same finding via controlled experimentation, as demonstrating this via an experiment might mean denying certain learners access to books!

Regression analysis

A regression analysis is logically very similar to correlation. However, it has more subtlety as it includes multiple variables. This allows us to estimate not just how one variable relates to another, but also how it compares to other variables, giving us an overview of what the strongest associations are.

In the last example about maths, let's imagine that you want to find out what will boost maths attainment, and reading is just one possibility that you have thought of. The regression analysis would allow the variables to be compared. For example, as well as reading/literacy scores, the researcher could look at the statistical effect of classroom relationships, a teacher's qualifications or experience, the classroom techniques or materials used, etc. This would allow the researcher to weigh up multiple factors that might affect attainment, and find out which are more strongly connected.

Again, though, it's worth noting that regression analysis still just shows a statistical relationship. Like correlation, it doesn't tell us why that relationship exists.

If you have never done a regression analysis before, it's best to be guided through it by a researcher with experience, and this book will not go into the option any further (but see the further reading at the end of the chapter). Because of its exploratory nature, it's an ideal choice for the first stage of a larger research project, or perhaps a Masters dissertation that could provide the foundation for a later PhD or EdD. Gaining data in this way, particularly if published (see Chapter 17) could provide the basis for a funding bid, making it easier to explore the findings in more depth.

Research project: one very simple project that you can do in order to practice using correlation and understand its limitations would be to compare attendance with scores on a class test.

How to do it: most classroom teachers will already have a note of attendance for each of their pupils, and this can easily be converted to a percentage. This is one of your co-variables. The second is their score on a relevant measure of attainment such as a class

---

test or mock exam. These can be entered onto a spreadsheet in two columns, and a scattergram generated with the click of a button.

Clearly there would be a rationale for hypothesising that pupils who go to class more often will get better grades. However, you can also anticipate some other factors. You may have a pupil with a chronic illness who misses a lot of classes but gets very good marks. Such a pupil will show up as an 'outlier' on the scattergram (far away from the line of best fit).

This project also demonstrates some of the tricky issues with cause and effect. Even if you do find that pupils who attend less get worse marks, is this actually a causal relationship? There could be other variables involved—for example, perhaps pupils with worse parental support or poorer motivation are likely to both attend less often and underachieve in class.

Concluding comments

Correlation is an essential tool for the teacher-researcher to know about. It's one of the more straightforward to put into practice, given that it can be used on data that you already have.

Perhaps even more importantly, it's useful for teachers to be able to recognise what a correlation means when reading about it in different contexts. Correlational findings are often poorly reported by the media, with cause and effect taken for granted, even when the data do not actually support such a conclusion. Understanding how correlation works, and the ways to interpret a finding such as a strong, weak, positive or negative correlation, will help in your development as a more critical consumer of research evidence.

Further reading

A fun and accessible way to explore the concept of regression analysis is 'The manga guide to regression analysis' (2016, No Starch Press) by Shin Takahashi.

Discussion questions

* What kind of numerical data do you already have or could you easily obtain?

* Most of the examples in this chapter concern classes of pupils. Can you think of any possible data sets about other situations that you could analyse—data on schools, for example?

* Can you think of a situation where might it be more ethical to conduct a correlation-based study rather than gathering primary (new) data on pupils?

Notes

1 There could be some confusion here if you speak to colleagues who are less research engaged than yourself—they may assume that 'primary/secondary data' refers to the schools involved (primary and secondary schools), so it is important to clarify.
2 Why not IV and DV again? This is because correlation studies cannot show causality, and the researcher therefore wants to avoid making misleading assumptions about which variable might causing a change in the other.
3 Goleman, D. (2006). *Emotional intelligence.* New York: Bantam.
4 Mayer, J. D., Salovey, P., Caruso, D. R., and Sitarenios, G. (2001). Emotional intelligence as a standard intelligence. *Emotion*, 1(3), 232–42.
5 Mavroveli, S., and Sanchez-Ruiz, M. J. (2011). Trait emotional intelligence influences on academic achievement and school behaviour. *British Journal of Educational Psychology*, 81, 112–134.
6 Perera, H., and DiGiacomo, M. (2013). The relationship of trait emotional intelligence with academic performance: A meta-analytic review. *Learning and Individual Differences*, 28, 20–33.
7 Mayer, J. D., Caruso, D. R., and Salovey, P. (1999). Emotional intelligence meets traditional standards for an intelligence. *Intelligence*, 27(4), 267–298.
8 Depending on the statistical test used, the data may need to be at least interval level, meaning that the gaps between different numbers (such as between 2 and 3 and between 4 and 5 on a scale) are equivalent in distance.

Quantitative methods

This chapter will highlight the key options available to the teacher-researcher when gathering numerical data, and will also explore data analysis.

We hear a lot in education nowadays about data—most of it bad. Reducing children's educational performance to a set of numbers is rightly seen as being overly simplistic, and potentially harmful if numbers are treated as labels expressing ability. The drive for large-scale data gathering has become almost synonymous with standardised testing/SAT programmes, and the issues with how and why these are used. Making decisions on the basis of huge data sets ('big data') is nowadays possible and attractive to some, but such decisions may fail to capture the nuances of individual classrooms.

These concerns shouldn't let us lose sight of the fact that data can be very useful to the researcher and their audience. Research methods that produce findings in the forms of numbers—collectively known as quantitative methods—are a set of tools, nothing more. As long as the meaning of a numerical finding is not overstated, it can be a useful way of summarising complex information, and can help us to get findings across to other people clearly.

A use for numbers

We are going to focus on **research methods**, that is, ways of gathering data. However, the term 'quantitative' does not refer to the research method but to the data. Quantitative data are based around numbers—measurements which provides an indication of how well a learner has done at a task, for example, or how much something has changed.

Like the pH number that tells you whether a substance is acidic or alkaline, they can provide something more objective than a verbal statement; reporting a pH level as 5.7 is preferable to 'it seems pretty acidic to me'. Critically, this form of data makes findings more easily compared. How do I know that my idea of 'the learners did well' is the same as someone else's, and how can I compare how well a class are performing to last year's cohort? If we use the same tests with standardised or percentage scores, then this is much easier to do.

The same point applies to comparing findings within one such study, such as finding out whether learners are scoring higher on a test of motivation or well-being after our intervention than they were before it.

Ways of gathering numerical data

The main research methods this chapter will focus on are:

- *Tests*: many experimental designs (see Chapter 9) involve giving a test or task of some kind. They may involve doing a test before and after an intervention so that scores can be compared, or under two different conditions. School tests provide naturally-occurring data of a similar type.

- **Questionnaires**: a questionnaire is a list of questions, either on paper or online, which gather written or typed responses.

- **Structured observations**: due to our experience of lesson observations, we perhaps don't always associate observations with research, or with numerical responses. However an observation which uses a numerical form of data gathering can be a good way of gaining objective (if sometimes quite shallow) data about pupils' actions in school.

Tests, tasks and scales

As every teacher knows, there are multiple ways of setting a test. In fact, just about any educational task could be set as a test, as long as there is some way of judging the outcome in a way that provides us with numerical data.

Most commonly, experimental research studies give participants a simple task which can be scored in a fairly objective way. For example, if something is taught, a multiple choice test might be given, allowing a percentage score to be obtained for each learner. In the case of a skill such as identifying the theme of a story, they may be tested before and after the lesson.

Laboratory research often devises such tasks in order to test a specific concept, but in a school context it might be best to maintain a high level of mundane realism, meaning that it would be better to use a task which is part of your normal practice and use that, rather than create something new.

Even something with a verbal response, such as a group discussion, could lead to numerical data—it could be judged on its duration, number of words used, accuracy of points made, number of people who contributed, etc. For younger participants, items such as pictures that they draw or the level of detail in mind maps[1] can be used as the basis of data gathering (see recommended reading).

Other tests and tasks which can generate quantitative data and could potentially form part of a research study include:

- Psychological scales (see PsyToolkit.org for an excellent library of scales that includes standardised tests of personality, happiness, procrastination, maths anxiety and many more).
- Reaction time (there are online games which can test this in fun ways).
- Apps which measure useful variables (e.g. sleep, number of steps walked, screen time, etc).
- IQ or working memory tests.

It's not always the case in research that participants are given any feedback on their responses—sometimes these are kept within the research team. In the classroom, however, you may well want to share the outcome with your pupils. This is absolutely fine, but some delay in sharing this may be necessary in order to ensure that you are not biasing the results of any follow up tasks. There are actually good scientific arguments that suggest that delaying feedback may actually be beneficial (see From the research, below)—a good excuse for taking your time when marking!

From the research

Key issue: feedback—how much, how often and how quickly? It is often assumed that feedback to learners should be detailed, and should be given immediately. This fits with the framework of formative assessment (or 'assessment for learning'—AfL), which states that the main purpose of assessments is to provide feedback which then guides future learning. In contrast, Veronica Yan and colleagues report that in laboratory psychology studies, feedback is often more effective if it is reduced and delayed.[2] So which is correct?

What the research says: the concept of feedback on learning links back to behaviourist psychology, a framework which investigated behaviour change on the basis of rewards and punishments. More recently, feedback has been seen as important when forming mental models of the world, and for self-regulation.

The issue is complicated by the fact that there are multiple types of feedback—from praise, to the outcome of a task (success or failure), to being given the right answer. It's therefore difficult to determine the effect of feedback across the board. If a learner is unknowingly making a simple mistake, it will be useful for the teacher to draw their attention to this soon, rather than having them repeat it (as it may become an automatic habit, as is the case with many spelling errors).

However, as Dylan Wiliam notes, the large majority of feedback given by teachers has little effect on achievement. One reason for this is that such feedback often takes the form of comments on written work or generalisations made to a class, and these are largely ignored by learners. A learner needs to feel motivated to receive and respond to the feedback[3]—perhaps by being in a state of uncertainty about how to complete a task or solve a problem.

One way to reconcile these ideas would be to say that rapid error correction is necessary during initial learning but that overall feedback on attainment often occurs too soon, such as the review of learning outcomes and filling in of exit passes that take place at the end of a lesson. Spacing such feedback out over time could benefit from the spacing effect (see Chapter 5), as it reminds learners of what they were working on before. Such delays also give learners more time to reflect and to tackle problems further by themselves.

Surveys

Quantitative data can also be gathered via surveys, meaning a research study that gathers data from a broad sample using a questionnaire. The questions will typically ask for simple factual answers, responses on a scale or choices from a selection of options. This allows you as the researcher to summarise the data numerically, for example by calculating an average answer or determining the percentage of people who chose each option (questionnaires could also ask more in-depth, open questions; see Chapter 12 for more information about qualitative data gathering).

A survey generally involves distributing a questionnaire to a wide and representative sample of participants. As such, it is useful to think about the most suitable method of distribution. Some of the main possibilities include:

- Posting the questionnaire to participants or putting it in a school/work pigeon hole.
- Handing the questionnaire out in person, e.g. during a class.

- Emailing the questionnaire as an attachment.
- An internet-based questionnaire which could be emailed or shared via social media.

One consideration when deciding what type of survey to do is the response rate. This means how many people complete the questionnaire. Some who start may give up and not complete it, possibly making their data useless:

- Questionnaires distributed via email and social media are typically looking for volunteers, and you can expect a low response rate. In order to account for this, you will need to find a way of making the message visible to a large number of people, and assume that a low percentage will complete it.
- Giving out a questionnaire in person, especially if time is allocated (for example, ten minutes before assembly begins), is likely to greatly increase the response rate. However, you should consider the issue of coercion (see Chapter 8)—will this mean that participants are effectively forced to take part in the research? In order to avoid this, they should have a reasonable alternative available to them, such as using the time for reading.

A survey is typically completed without the researcher having any direct input (in contrast to an interview), and so it must be very easy for the participants to understand the questions. There should be no risk of misunderstanding. One of the main advantages of using surveys to gather quantitive data is that they can be distributed to a large sample, and still analysed relatively easily.

Case study: writing a questionnaire

Consider the following case which explores the use of questionnaires by a teacher-researcher:

Arya is a primary school teacher who is considering running a survey study, making use of a questionnaire. However, her views on how best to do this differ from those of her colleagues.

Arya works with the upper primary age range, and is concerned about the loss of motivation as pupils reach the end of primary school. She agrees to study this together with two colleagues, and decides to write a questionnaire asking pupils about their motivation. She drafts several questions such as 'On a scale of 1–10, how much do you like school?'. However, when she shows the questionnaire to her colleagues, they say that it is ambiguous. They suggest that they use pupils' own comments that have been provided in real class surveys, and ask pupils to agree or disagree with these prior comments.

As this example shows, it can be problematic to write your own questionnaire from scratch. For starters, it is a difficult skill to word questions clearly, and bias in the wording is likely to creep in, with questions subtly leading participants towards the answers that you want or expect.

Even if your wording is flawless, a new questionnaire has not been validated, meaning that it is hard for the research community as a whole to compare its findings to other work. What does a high score on the questionnaire actually show? And are all of the questions tapping into a single variable (in this case, motivation)? It will often be better to use an existing questionnaire, if available, because these have already been statistically validated, and flaws in wording will have been ironed out.

Valid questions

As raised in the case study, the wording of questions is important. They need to gain good data, in that responses will reflect the variable under investigation, thereby helping to answer the research question. Consider the following items:

> How regularly do you revise? Often/Quite often/Rarely/
> Not at all
> How many hours in total do you spend studying for a typical exam?
> How many hours did you spend revising last weekend?

Each of the questions in the last box has its pros and cons. The first, in particular, is quite vague (what counts as revising? Which subjects are we talking about?) although it does allow a reasonable breadth of responses. The second is more specific, but it could be quite hard to answer—will learners even know how many hours they spend on revision overall? And what is a typical exam, anyway? The third question is more specific still, and more likely to get an accurate answer. The problem is that it is so specific, it doesn't necessarily capture behaviour that reflects a participant's normal habits. For example, perhaps last weekend was unusual due to an event that meant they didn't spend any hours revising at all, meaning that the question would not provide a valid measure of a learner's study habits.

If it is clear, accessible and easy to answer, respondents will also be more likely to complete and return the questionnaire.

Some general design points for suitable questions include:

- Avoid leading questions.
- Avoid technical jargon.
- Avoid ambiguity.
- Avoid emotive language.

In short, questions should be as neutral as possible, and seek information that respondents can reasonably be expected to know. You can write your own questions successfully if you are going to ask for simple objective information such as what subject a person teaches, or how long they have been teaching for. If you want to find out about a complex theoretical construct such as motivation or growth mindset via a survey, it would be best to use an existing questionnaire.

If an appropriate questionnaire does not exist or is not freely available, one approach that limits the difficulties of suitable wording could be to access older statements—for example statements as part of a previous year's end-of-course feedback—and combine these with a Likert scale (as was suggested by the colleagues in the case study on p. 158). A **Likert scale** is a questionnaire format which shows verbal items and asks people to agree or disagree with these, typically on a 5-point or 7-point scale:

- Strongly disagree: 1
- Disagree: 2
- Weakly disagree: 3
- Neutral: 4
- Weakly agree: 5
- Agree: 6
- Strongly agree: 7

It is important to balance positive and negative statements, so that agreeing with the underlying concept sometimes leads to 'agree' answers and sometimes to 'disagree' answers. This is done by phrasing some positive and some negative statements. For example, if you wanted to find out views on making Psychology a mandatory part of the primary school curriculum, you might present items like these:

1) Primary pupils could benefit from learning about memory and stress.
2) Primary pupils are too young to learn about mental health issues.

As can be seen, someone who supported the idea under investigation would agree with statement 1, and disagree with statement 2.[4]

Likert scales are relatively quick and easy to answer and can gather a lot of data. However, it may be necessary to include some open questions in your questionnaire. For example, if surveying teachers, it may be necessary to ask what subject they teach, or how many years it is since they trained.

Finally, it's worth noting that many surveys made by novice researchers are very long, perhaps in a desire to gather as much data as possible—casting the net wide in order to catch something of interest. A good questionnaire is as short as it can be (this is also more ethical, minimising any time wasted), meaning that it asks the necessary questions but nothing more. Short questionnaires are also more likely to be completed, increasing both the response rate and, consequently, the validity of results (as they are not completed only by the most conscientious participants).

For any item in your questionnaire, ask yourself whether the responses would appear in the method section or results section of an eventual research write-up. Will the findings make any difference to your analysis? Do you really need to know this information? If not, the question should be cut out.

Observations

An **observation** is a way of gathering data by simply watching and recording people's behaviour as it happens. It lends itself to gathering data on things that can be seen externally, such as how long a pupil stays on task or their classroom behaviour, but is less useful for finding out about things like thoughts or emotions. It can be usefully combined with other means of gathering data, such as tests and questionnaires.

There are various ways in which we could conduct observations of research participants. Two main possibilities are:

- **Naturalistic observation**: conducting an observation of a real life situation, without interfering.
- **Structured observation**: setting up a task for people to do and then observing them as they do it.

As will perhaps be obvious, there are differences in the data that might be recorded via these two options, and each has its own strengths and weaknesses. You will also have experienced both already in your own life; a naturalistic observation is what happens in typical school observations—an observer enters the room and observes a normal class, taking notes without interacting. A structured observation is what happens at many job interviews—you are given a (somewhat artificial) task to do, such as giving a presentation, and are observed while doing it.

Clearly, structured observations are inherently more artificial, but they have the advantage that they prompt a particular behaviour to occur. If you want to observe conflict, for example, it could be very time-consuming to just sit and wait for it to happen, and much quicker to give a group of participants a competitive board game to play during your observation.

There are of course some weaknesses with observation as a research method:

- The observer effect: similar to the researcher effect, this is where the presence of the observer biases the behaviour of the people who are being observed.
- Ethics, invasion of privacy: some observations are intrusive, and people may well react negatively if they weren't told in advance that they were going to be observed.

In theory, the observer effect could be reduced by making the observation secret, but it is unethical to do so. Another way around it is to get the participants used to the observer. You will have noticed that when a new person (e.g. a student teacher) comes into class, it will affect behaviour, but that after a couple of lessons with that person in the room things return to normal. The same principle can be applied when researching—giving participants time to get used to an observer. A video camera could be even less obtrusive, though some time to habituate to it would still be beneficial.

Observation schedules

What is on the other side of the clipboard? Typically an observer doesn't just have a blank sheet of paper on which they take notes.

An **observation schedule** is a list of things that the observer is looking for during the session. There are multiple possible ways that these can be organised. Some of the most relevant to education researchers include:

- Time sampling of behaviour: here, the observer notes what is occurring at regular intervals, such as noting the most predominant behaviour in evidence once per minute.

- Checklist of behaviour: here, the observer checks behaviours off as and when they occur, recording each one only once.

- Checklist with tally marks: as above, but the observer adds to the tally every time the behaviour occurs.

In any case, the researcher will want to give some thought in advance to what behaviours they are looking for. A pilot study can be helpful in order to finalise the options that will be included.

It will also be necessary to establish which individuals the observer is watching. In the classroom, the observer could observe one pupil, or a group or even the whole class. It is clearly harder to gather data on a large group, however, and the level of detail might have to be reduced accordingly.

Inter-observer reliability

To ensure really good quality observation data, studies often use more than one observer watching the same behaviour. Here, the two sets of data can be compared. If they are very similar, the research has achieved high **inter-observer reliability**.

There are various reasons that inter-observer reliability might be low. The main ones are difficulty of the observer's task (too much to watch), the observation schedule being complex or hard to use, subjectivity of some of the categories (e.g. a checklist item such as 'bad behaviour'), and lack of training on the part of the observers. All of these can be remedied with further planning and preparation.

Analysis

Summarising your data

When dealing with scores from tests or with numerical data from certain types of observations, the first step is often to use descriptive statistics—mathematical means of summarising the data in just a few numbers. The key statistics are probably familiar to you:

- The mean: the arithmetic average, calculated by adding up all scores and dividing by 'n' i.e. the number of scores.
- The mode: the most common or popular score, a form of 'average' that is not distorted by extreme values, and is also helpful when data are based around categories such that a mean cannot be calculated (e.g. responses to 'who is your favourite teacher?').
- The median: the midpoint of the data, obtained by putting scores in order, low to high, and finding the one in the centre. Again this can be useful if your data include outliers.

These ways of showing the average don't fully capture the data, though, as they don't show how spread out the scores were. Measures of dispersion show how widely data are spread:

- The range: this is simply the difference between the lowest and highest scores. It is limited in that it doesn't reflect the distribution of the other data.
- The standard deviation: this shows the typical amount by which the scores in the distribution differ from the mean. The calculation is based on finding the difference between each score and the mean, and then calculating the average of these differences, and can easily be done on a spreadsheet. An advantage is that all data are included in the calculation.

These statistics are also useful when analysing surveys—for example, you may wish to find the mean age of respondents, or the most common (modal) teaching subject.

Analysing survey responses

For other types of survey questions, you may need to calculate a percentage. For example, what percentage of your respondents said that they read research articles on a weekly basis?

As discussed earlier, Likert scale items should include a mixture of negative and positive items, so you will need to 'flip' some of the answers before your analysis. This means that the Likert scores are reversed, so that for these questions a 7 becomes a 1, a 6 becomes a 2, and so on. After you have done so, you will be able to analyse the responses further.

One way to analyse responses to a single Likert item is using the mode. This tells us the most common response. You could also state what percentage agreed or strongly agreed with a particular statement on your Likert scale. It's best not to use the mean when analysing a single item. This is because it doesn't make sense or tell us anything meaningful to find the average of terms such as 'strongly agree', 'neutral' and 'disagree'.

When it comes to analysing the scale as a whole, you may be able to group items into 'agree' and 'disagree' overall for a particular concept within the scale. It's then possible to carry out a *chi-square* statistical test to determine whether one of these is chosen more often than would be expected by chance.

Statistical hypothesis testing

Statistics can also be used to determine whether the results of two tests differ from each other in a way that is considered significant—that is, it is unlikely to have occurred by chance. This is known as *statistical hypothesis testing*.

The key idea is that any finding could have occurred by chance, but the more unlikely this is to happen, the more certain we can be that our result reflects a real difference.

Imagine that you wanted to know whether a coin was weighted towards heads rather than being fairly balanced. You could toss the coin ten times and get heads eight out of ten times. Does this prove that it is weighted? Not really. However, it's unlikely that an average coin would have produced this result. Here, our null hypothesis is that the coin is fair (and we would therefore expect five heads and five tails). We would use a statistical test to determine how unlikely it is that a fair coin would produce eight heads by chance (as may be obvious, tossing the coin more times would give us a better set of data—a larger sample is preferable in quantitative research).

Statistical hypothesis testing compares your finding with the presumed probability of the result occurring by chance. The usual threshold is 5%, that is, the result is accepted as significant if there is a less than 5% chance of gaining a result that extreme if the null hypothesis were actually true (for example, that the classroom intervention that you are testing actually made no difference).

There are various statistical tests that can be used to calculate a **p-value**, a number which will then be compared against a standard value based on the type of statistical test you have used and your sample size. If your p-value exceeds this standard value, the result is significant.

There are a large number of such tests, and which one you use depends on the data. For experimental designs—where you are looking at the effect of an independent variable on a dependent variable—the choice depends on:

- How many variables you are testing (one independent variable or several).
- Whether the scores come from the same group or two groups (e.g. the same class trying two tasks, or two separate classes).
- Whether the data are normally distributed (fitting a bell-shaped curve, with middle values common and extreme values uncommon).
- Whether you take a single measurement of the dependent variable, or do 'before and after' measurements.

Two of the most useful to know about are as follows:

- *Paired samples t-test*: this can be used when you are comparing two sets of data from the same people—for example, if your class tried a maths test with and without music.

- *ANOVA*: the two-way ANOVA or 'analysis of variance' is one of the most common statistical tests in psychology and can be applied to educational experiments too. It is used when we need to find out the effects of more than one independent variable and whether these variables interact.

This book will not explain the calculation of these tests, on the basis that reading a short explanation in a book is not sufficient to fully understand how and why you do them (not to mention learning to use the software for running the calculations). If you don't already have experience with statistics, it would be a good idea to find a colleague who can explain these tests to you (and it's also useful to read research papers that have used the same statistical tests). There are many books and useful resources online which will walk you through the steps of various tests (see further reading at the end of this chapter).

In general, it would be a good idea for any teacher-researcher to link up with a suitably skilled colleague, such as a member of the maths department in your school. Teachers with a background in science and social science subjects will also have done advanced statistics during their degrees, and may be able to help you. This is just one of the many areas in which fruitful research partnerships can develop if two or more people have complementary skills (or, perhaps, with researchers outside of your school).

Graphs

Quantitative results lend themselves well to being displayed in tables and graphs, and these will make an academic poster, blog post or research article much more visually interesting.

A bar chart is very helpful for displaying responses to Likert scales (percentages who agreed/disagreed etc), or for comparing the scores on tests under two conditions in an experiment or RCT. A line graph is often clearer than a bar graph if you want to show the interaction between two independent variables (see Chapter 9).

There are various other graphs that can be used, one of which (scattergrams for correlation) was discussed earlier in this book. It can be helpful to look at previous research studies to see how similar sets of data to your own tend to be presented.

Research project: it would be a good idea to start with a short, simple survey that would allow you to gather some data without too many ethical issues. As such, why not find out more about how your colleagues engage with research? Finding this out could provide some of the groundwork for establishing a research community in your school.

How to do it: the survey could be distributed online, but following the point made above about response rate, you may get more data (and more representative data) if you choose to hand it out on paper at a staff event, for example while teachers are waiting for a CPD event to begin.

In terms of the questions, it may be best to ask simple closed questions about how long they have been teaching, how long they have been in the school, and how frequently they read research articles/TES/Impact. You could use an existing questionnaire, or have a Likert-style section asking colleagues to agree or disagree with statements like:

'I think that research awareness is fundamental to teaching professionalism.'

'I don't have time to engage more with research than I do at present.'

'I still have a lot to learn from research.'

'I would enjoy carrying out my own independent research project.'

'I would need some detailed ethics guidance before running my own classroom research.'

(continued)

169

(continued)

Statements could be sourced from written articles about teacher research engagement, or by doing an interview with a colleague as a pilot study and using anonymised statements as stimuli.

The findings should be kept anonymous and this should be made clear to participants, but it might be good to ask for names, and/or to ask them to opt in to receiving further communication and support, meaning that people who state they are interested in doing a research project could be offered help (see also Chapter 14).

Concluding comments

This chapter has focused on three of the most important and widely used methods of gathering quantitative data: tests and tasks (closely associated with experiments), questionnaires and observations.

However, even if you are drawn to quantitative data gathering and analysis, it is worth considering whether qualitative methods would be useful to consider as an alternative—or in addition. For example, perhaps you could supplement statistical data on how well a learning technique worked with a focus group which asked pupils what they felt about it, and whether they enjoyed it. This can make for a richer approach to data gathering, particularly for longer projects. Qualitative methods are discussed in the next chapter.

Further reading

'Statistics without tears' by Derek Rowntree (2000, Penguin Books) is an excellent starting point for understanding statistics for those inexperienced with the maths involved. Subtitled 'An introduction for non-mathematicians', the book does an excellent job of explaining the principles behind statistical processes such as the standard deviation and standard error, without getting bogged down in the calculations.

'Research methods for understanding professional learning' by Kate Wall and Elaine Hall (2019, Bloomsbury) is a very useful guide to these and other methods, and includes a unique section on visual methodologies.

Discussion questions

◉ Under what circumstances might giving a practical written test be an inappropriate method of gathering data?

◉ A teacher wants to observe the effect of an intervention on her class's behaviour, but is concerned that bringing in an observer would bias the results. What solutions to this problem might you suggest?

◉ A teacher aims to conduct his research by writing a long questionnaire for pupils, asking about their learning habits and how they learn best. What feedback might you give him?

Notes

1 Wall, K., Hall, E., and Woolner, P. (2012). Visual methodology: previously, now and in the future. *International Journal of Research & Method in Education*, 35(3), 223–226.
2 Yan, V. X., Clark, C. M., and Bjork, R. A. (2016). Memory and metamemory considerations in the instruction of human beings revisited: Implications for optimizing online learning. In J. C. Horvath, J. Lodge, and J. A. C. Hattie (Eds). *From the laboratory to the classroom: Translating the learning sciences for teachers* (pp. 61–78). Abingdon, UK: Routledge.
3 Shute, V. J. (2008). Focus on formative feedback. *Review of Educational Research*, 78(1), 153–189.
4 You can see a good example of this in Psychology Today's 'hardiness' test, here: https://bit.ly/2SbvRRo

Qualitative methods

Qualitative research focuses on verbal, descriptive data. It is associated with certain research methods—in particular, interviews. This contrasts with methods that gather numerical data (the quantitative methods described in the previous chapter).

Many teachers are attracted by qualitative methods. This may be in part because they are put off by the statistics associated with quantitative data, or because qualitative data gathering seems to ask questions more directly, and to explore issues in greater depth. Here, we will look at two of the main methods for gathering verbal data—open interviews and focus groups—and consider their uses and their shortcomings. As we will see, both are helpful and accessible ways of gathering data, but they should not be seen as 'easy' research, and they come with their own challenges. The use of questionnaires and observations to gather qualitative data and the use of secondary data will also be considered.

Qualitative data

As with the quantitative methods (see previous chapter), the term 'qualitative' does not refer to the research method but to the data. Qualitative data relates to the qualities or characteristics of a thing, rather than measuring that thing on a scale. For example, you may be asking *how* something has changed, rather than *how much* it changed.

In practice, this means that gathering qualitative data is often more nuanced and subjective than the quantitative alternatives. It may be appropriate in situations where existing theories suggest that an issue is not about less versus more, but that there are various dimensions to consider.

One example of qualitative research in practice could be a study of how pupils react to an exam or test. Granted, it would be possible to ask them to rate how content they were with the test on a scale from 1–10, but doing so would surely not fully capture their emotions and thoughts, and arguably would not really be a valid measure of any single variable. In short, their reaction to the test will not be a case of less or more; instead, there are numerous possible ways that a person might feel about their exam, best described in words.

Cross-over with quantitative methods

The research method itself (interviews, surveys and so on) can be seen as a tool for gathering data. It's not restricted to one type of data in particular. Two of the methods discussed in the previous chapter are also widely used in qualitative research:

- Surveys: participants can be asked open questions (for example, 'how did you feel about the exam?'), allowing them to express answers in natural language. This way they are unconstrained by researcher-selected options, in contrast to closed questions or Likert scales where they have to choose from a selection of possibilities.

- Observations: again, an observation could gather either kind of data. If it involves verbal descriptions of behaviour that is being observed, then it will generate qualitative data, perhaps in addition to quantitative measures. In the classroom, the latter could be used to gather information about an entire class (such as how many put their hand up during the lesson), while the former would be better suited to recording information on one specific pupil at a time.

In both cases, the researcher takes a different approach when seeking qualitative data. Instead of placing an emphasis on getting as much data as possible, qualitative research—as the name implies—emphasises high quality, richly meaningful data.

So, for example, one reason for using a survey rather than an interview to ask open questions is that it will be easier to get a lot of responses. But many qualitative researchers would argue that such responses will be of low quality, they will be divorced from a natural context (such as a conversation), and respondents may not fully understand what they are being asked or why.

Interviews

The key characteristic of the interview is that questions are asked face-to-face. In comparison to distributing a written survey, this makes the research more time-consuming to carry out, but allows for misunderstandings to be clarified. It is ideal for situations where a small number of people are going to be questioned, and where the research is exploratory—you don't really know yet what kind of answers you are going to find.

Individual interviews are time-consuming to run, and the data from open questions is harder to analyse, but these limitations can be offset by the unique ability of this research method to delve into an individual's thoughts, and to try to see an issue from their point of view.

Interviews tend to be classified into three broad groups, and it's useful to think at an early stage about which type you wish to conduct:

- A *structured interview* uses a fixed list of questions. It is therefore quite similar to a survey, except conducted face-to-face. The interviewer will not go beyond the questions on the list, except to make clarifications. They will typically use mainly closed questions.

- A *semi-structured interview* begins with a set list of questions, but allows the interviewer some freedom. The interviewer may ask the respondent to elaborate on some answers. There is enough structure to ensure that the content of answers sticks to the same broad issues, and the personality of the interviewer doesn't play a major role.

An *unstructured interview* does not stick to a fixed list of questions, allowing the interviewer to vary their questioning depending on how a participant responds. Many open-ended questions may be used. However, responses are open to interpretation by the researcher, and there is a danger of researcher bias.

The choice of interview type depends largely on the purpose of the research. Structured interviews facilitate some quantitative analysis, but fail to take advantage of one of the main strengths of interviews—the ability to explore a participant's unique perspective. With unstructured interviews, it is hard to make generalisations across a group of participants, as they will all have talked about different things.

In many ways, then, the semi-structured interview provides the best of both worlds—some standardisation to make comparisons across participants possible, while still affording the chance to record depth and detail in the answers.

Quality of interview data

Although it may seem natural to take notes during an interview, the best approach for research purposes is to digitally record the interview (with the participant's consent, of course). This allows you to focus on questioning without being distracted by trying to take down notes, and ensures that answers recorded are word-for-word the same as what a participant actually said.

Of course, this only ensures that the data are an accurate record of what was said—it doesn't ensure that what was said is actually true! It's always possible that participants may distort the truth in order to look good to the interviewer. This is an example of social desirability bias. Another flaw to consider is that the interviewee simply doesn't know the right answer—rather than lying, they may make a genuine mistake. Their response could reflect assumptions, prejudices and false memories, rather than knowledge (see Chapter 6).

These issues don't reflect flaws in methodology itself, but rather in the planning process behind it. Can participants be reasonably expected to know what they are being asked about? For example, imagine you were to ask A-Level students about their study habits, and how they study best. It's likely that questions about when and how they study will lead to some errors, due to flaws in memory. They may also make false assumptions about their own learning process—for example, stating that they learn best by re-reading and highlighting texts, when psychological research would suggest otherwise (see Chapter 3). That is to say, their metacognitive knowledge about their learning might be flawed.

From the research

<u>Key issue</u>: what is **metacognition**? It can be defined as thinking about thinking (usually, thinking about your own thinking). It can include such issues as awareness of your own thought processes, or the way that you monitor and plan your own decision making. Learners and interview participants alike might be asked to reflect on their own thoughts, decisions and plans, and be asked questions such as 'why did you do this?'. But can they do so accurately?

<u>What the research says</u>: a traditional model of human thinking, popular until the 20th Century, was that humans are the rational animal. Human thought was seen as essentially logical, and so economists and political decision makers assumed that incentives could be used to modify behaviour.

However, researchers into human decision making have repeatedly shown that people's thinking is biased and illogical in multiple ways. Psychologists have shown that delusions and obsessions are hard to shift, and that people's judgements and memories are biased towards themselves and against members of other groups. And economists Tversky and Kahneman showed that people tend to be insensitive to issues such as probability and sample size when making judgements.[1]

What's more, people tend to lack a metacognitive awareness of their own ignorance. As researcher David Dunning puts it,

"People are destined not to know where the solid land of their knowledge ends and the slippery shores of their ignorance begin."[2] And research into cognitive dissonance suggests that people often act first, and then rethink their beliefs in order to be consistent with those actions. This can bias the way they perceive and reflect on their own actions.[3] It might be best if interview responses were assumed to be replete with rationalisations and errors.

Focus groups

Another major method of gathering qualitative data is the use of a focus group. This is where a group of people are brought together to discuss a particular issue as a (fairly) natural discussion. First developed for use in market research by asking groups to respond to planned products or adverts, it has become a mainstream means of data gathering in social science.

The focus group are often, though not always, asked to respond to a particular stimulus. In classroom-based research, they could be asked to view a section of a lesson or some learning materials and then have a discussion. The group are usually chosen to be as diverse as possible, but may all be members of the target population that is of interest, such as a particular year group. Indeed, it could be difficult to stimulate a natural conversation if a group is composed of pupils of several different ages.

In essence, a focus group is rather similar to an unstructured interview, but conducted with a group rather than an individual. Why would this be done? There are three major reasons:

- It is more efficient to ask several people at once rather than interviewing them separately. With a group of ten people, for example, it would be time-consuming to plan and conduct ten separate interviews, when a single session of the same length could gather responses from all of them at once.

- One person's responses could stimulate ideas and reactions in the others. The focus group therefore doesn't just generate individual responses of people saying how they feel—it also provides a rich text, with interactions. If one person says that they like something, we can quickly see whether their peers agree or disagree. This also helps to tackle the issue that participants in unstructured interviews can end up focusing on very different things from one another (see Interviews, p. 174).

● The focus group provides something that resembles a natural inter-action. This could make it preferable to the relatively artificial stim-ulus of an anonymous questionnaire.

There are, however, some downsides to focus groups. In social psy-chology, it is well established that people tend to conform to a majority in a one-off group setting, especially if the others are unanimous and if the minority individual is not sure of themselves.[4] This means that we may gain a misleading sense of group agreement and harmony that masks any dissenting opinions, with a small number of forceful person-alities tending to dominate.

Also, the responses of other participants can't be planned in advance, so unlike a structured or semi-structured interview, it's difficult to know what direction the discussion will go in, and it's very hard to replicate it.

Case study: how can we improve clubs and societies?

Most schools have a selection of extra-curricular (or 'co-curricular') activities which are regularly offered to pupils, including sports, hobbies, creative arts, charity activities and so forth. But what is the best way to structure these, and how should they be offered? This school decided to ask the pupils themselves, using a focus group:

Two pastoral teachers and a school deputy head from a main-stream secondary school collaborated on a research project to gauge pupils' views of extra-curricular provision. Together they came up with a set of options, including the status quo and three alternative models. Volunteer pupils were sought out among two year groups, and from these a group of eight was selected at random. One lunchtime, each pupil was given ten minutes to look at the suggestions individually, and they were then put into a group, sitting round a table. The group were given a list of questions to consider and discuss, such as 'Which model would take up the most time in the school day?', or 'Which model would be most convenient for you?'. Pupils were given twenty minutes to work through all of the questions; lunch and drinks were provided. All three teacher-researchers watched from the side and took notes as the pupils talked.

During the discussion, one of the older pupils took charge of the list of questions and acted as an informal leader. He read each question out loud, and several others offered their opinion. As the discussion went on, three of the pupils became quiet, looking at their watches. The others each answered most of the questions, and where there were differences, the leader summed up his view of the group decision in a loud voice.

The advantages and disadvantages of the focus group come across strongly from this example. With individual interviews, everyone has an equal chance to speak, and it is perhaps easier to get a range of responses. Here the interaction was more natural, but that brings with it certain problems, with some group members tending to dominate and others becoming more withdrawn. The presence of the teachers could have affected the flow of the discussion and pupils' willingness to speak. It's also possible that the teachers each had their own biases, and their notes may not have been a fair reflection of the different voices among the group. A better alternative would have been to record and transcribe the discussion.

Other sources of data

There are some other ways of gathering qualitative data. Another source that could be considered is to ask participants to write reflective journals/logs: here, research participants write a daily or weekly reflection (in school or in their own time) which can later be analysed. Similarly, they could be asked to comment on their homework, make mind maps, copy up their revision schedule . . . The list goes on.

There are also many sources of qualitative data that already exist, without you having to generate new responses at all. Thinking back to the chapter on correlation (Chapter 10), you will recall that researchers sometimes use secondary data—data that already exists in some form, such as your records of attendance and test scores in your classes. In a similar way, you can consider some of the vast amount of verbal data available to you, just waiting to be gathered and analysed. This might include:

- A headteacher's daily speeches at assemblies.
- Lesson plans.
- Workbooks or handouts.
- Posts on Twitter or Instagram (if public).
- YouTube videos and vlogs.
- School newsletters.
- Text on a school's website.
- News articles about the school or about education.

Bear in mind that the same ethical issues of confidentiality and consent still apply. You shouldn't analyse colleagues' or pupils' emails without their consent, for example, but could analyse something that was already in the public domain such as a departmental workbook or a news article.

Next we will consider how to process the data (if necessary), in order to get it ready for analysis.

Transcribing the data

Some methods of qualitative data gathering (e.g. open questions in a survey) provide you with written data which is ready for further analysis. However, for a recorded interview or focus group, a further step is needed before this: **transcription**. This is where you convert the spoken, recorded file into a written text.

Transcription is a fairly easy skill to learn, but is very time-consuming. Many researchers pay for this to be done by a specialist—it is relatively inexpensive, and this can be a good use of any research funding that you have obtained. In line with what has previously said about teachers' time to engage with research (see Chapter 2), it's one task that you can easily cut out of your schedule.

However if you do decide to transcribe recordings yourself, bear the following in mind:

- Transcriptions should be a faithful, word-for-word record of what was said, not a summary.
- However, you don't need to transcribe filler words such as 'um'.
- Anything inaudible can be replaced with '[inaudible]'.
- Any major errors in grammar that might look like a mistake when reading the transcript could be labelled with '[sic]'.
- Allow at least 4–5 hours per hour of recording. You may need to play each section several times, or slow down the speed of the recording to better understand it.

Analysis of qualitative data

Having obtained a text, either directly or via transcription, you are now ready to analyse this data.

Or rather, you should be. Because data analysis is not something that should be left until after you have the data in front of you. Hopefully you give this some thought at the planning stage (see Chapter 7).

Background reading is often one of the best sources here—what kind of data have previous studies gathered, and how did they analyse it? If it worked for the experienced researchers in your field, it may well be suitable for you, too.

Imagine that you are conducting research into teacher stress and workload. Some of the main forms of qualitative data analysis that you could try include:

Thematic analysis

Thematic analysis involves coding the text according to themes or categories, usually ones that you have decided are important based on your prior research or a prominent theory. For example, if you had previously read that stress results mainly from workload, then you might choose to ask interview questions about workload pressures, and then to code results according to which pressures (marking, admin etc) were mentioned. Conclusions could be drawn on the basis of the prevalence of these themes (which are the most commonly discussed sources of stress), or how they interact with other variables (for example, experienced teachers are stressed by admin while new teachers are stressed by lesson planning). Sometime colour coding can be helpful to help make these themes visually obvious as you go through the text.

Narrative analysis

A limitation of thematic analysis is that it is researcher-led—that is, the researcher imposes their chosen framework onto the text. In a *narrative analysis*, the text is analysed on the respondent's terms, with their views and priorities leading the way. For example, if you were interviewing teachers about stress and they told you that the thing that stressed them most was management deadlines, you could use this as a theme with which to analyse data. This approach lends itself well to using a focus group or pilot study to identify key issues, and then following up with semi-structured interviews in order to explore these in more depth. Once suitable issues have been identified, the analysis can proceed in quite a similar way to thematic analysis.

It may occur to you, as discussed (see From the research on p. 176). that participants' narratives may not always be accurate representations of reality. Indeed, this is a facet of narrative analysis—trying to untangle the various influences, such as false memories, social assumptions and so on—that will impact on the real, factual picture.

Emergent coding

With this option, you avoid looking for particular themes in the text in advance (either based on the researcher's or participants' views), but instead wait and see what you might find. Themes may emerge as you read—for example you may notice that unexpectedly, lots of the teachers describe how their family lives influence their approach to managing stress. An emergent coding approach avoids making any prior assumptions, drawing on theory or the perspective of the participant(s), and instead goes purely on the basis of the text as it stands. In terms of methodology, this approach lends itself well to using secondary data, because interview questions often have underlying assumptions which can accidentally impose a theoretical framework. It could also fit well with asking participants to keep journals.

As can be seen with the references to 'coding', the main ways of analysing qualitative data involve finding out what the main variables are, and how they interact. In that respect, qualitative research is not so very different from quantitative. The main difference is that researchers who prefer qualitative research tend to believe (at least for their areas of interest) that variables can't meaningfully be separated from their real context.

Research project: a project which would make the best use of the strengths of the semi-structured interview could involve interviewing teachers and/or pupils about their perceptions of an

(continued)

(continued)

aspect of behaviour relating to school life. One such area is sleep; it has been recognised in recent years that pupil sleep quality is declining, and that this could affect both mental health and learning. Qualitative research could be done to ask the question: what causes pupils to get poor sleep?

How to do it: as noted above, the methodology links to the type of analysis that you want to carry out, and you may already have a good idea of what the main factors impacting on sleep are. However, it might also be a good idea to hear from the pupils themselves, as everyone is unique, and there could be issues that are particular to your location.

You could begin by selecting some secondary data in the form of a text, speech, article or parental blog post about the issue. Emergent coding could be used to identify the main issues that were raised, with key quotes identified. This could be followed up with a focus group, asking a small group of older pupils to comment on some of the issues raised. It would be interesting, when analysing the data, to see whether pupils raise different concerns from those found in the original text.

Concluding comments

This has been a fairly brief run through of some of the main methods of gathering qualitative data. If you want to make qualitative research your speciality and pursue publication, it is recommended that you refer to a specialist text (see further reading).

It's also worth noting here that all of the issues around evaluating findings apply just as much to qualitative research. Issues such as variables and validity of data may be harder to perceive with texts, but they still exist! For example, if you are using qualitative data to investigate teacher professionalism, can you be sure that the questions you are asking about professionalism are actually a valid way of measuring it, or could they be biased? And although direct replication is not always possible (e.g. when using secondary qualitative data), findings do need to be followed up so that they begin to contribute to a bigger picture of what is happening in your educational context.

It's always worth bearing in mind with qualitative research that the data gathered can easily be biased by misconceptions and flaws in memory. In the research project (see p. 183), for example, pupils may have heard that things like screen time and sugary snacks are bad for sleep, and therefore focus their answers on these. But believing something doesn't make it true. Qualitative research is often more useful in finding out about attitudes and beliefs in education than about the underlying processes themselves.

Further reading

For a more in-depth exploration of qualitative methods and data analysis, 'The qualitative dissertation in education: A guide for integrating research and practice' by Karri Holley and Michael Harris (2019, Routledge) is very helpful.

Discussion questions

- What is an open question?
- People do not always have full awareness of what they did and why they did it. Their memories may be incomplete or biased, and they may be unsure of their own motivations. How do these issues affect the use of interviews?
- If you were running a semi-structured interview in partnership with a research colleague, what would you do to prepare? Where and when would the interviews be conducted? And how would you keep the responses confidential and secure?
- In what situations might you choose to use a naturalistic observation to gather qualitative data?

Notes

1 Tversky, A., and Kahneman, D. (1974). Judgment under uncertainty: Heuristics and biases. *Science*, 185(4157), 1124–1131.
2 Dunning, D. (2011). The Dunning–Kruger effect: On being ignorant of one's own ignorance. In Zanna, M., and Olson, J. (Eds.) *Advances in experimental social psychology*, Vol 44 (pp. 247–296) (p. 250). New York: Academic Press.
3 Festinger, L. (1957). *A theory of cognitive dissonance*. Stanford, California: Stanford University Press.
4 Asch, S. E. (1955). Opinions and social pressure. *Scientific American*, 193(5), 31–35.

Research into your subject area

There is no rule which says that being a research-engaged teacher can only relate to educational research. Another option, instead of or in addition to engaging with educational research, would be to develop a subject-based research profile. This chapter looks at how a teacher can pursue areas of research in their own subject discipline, developing themselves as a leading expert in their field.

Research also plays a huge role in the teaching of subjects across the curriculum. It is commonplace for school pupils to carry out research projects at various points in their school careers—perhaps most notably, though not exclusively, in the sciences and social sciences. We will explore how pupils, too, can go beyond the basic requirements of their courses and begin to explore topics creatively, and how teachers and pupils can work together on research projects.

Where this chapter refers to discrete curriculum subjects such as Maths or Psychology, primary or early years teachers will be able to identify associated areas of the curriculum (e.g. maths for primary; pupil mental health, etc) to focus on. It's also worth noting that a pupil age group and its associated behavioural, social and cognitive changes could be a research area in itself.

Specialists and generalists

An immediate barrier to engaging as a researcher of your teaching subject is that a school or college teacher is typically something of a generalist compared to the specialists who populate the HE sector. For example, in science, a university lecturer might spend most of their time researching a highly specific area of Physics, and even if they are teaching new undergraduates they would tend to stick to their own particular area, such as optics or energy. In contrast, school-based teachers are expected to teach courses which cover every aspect of Physics, and, indeed, to teach other sciences at a basic level to younger pupils. For primary teachers, things are more challenging still—in many cases, primary teachers are expected to know about science in addition to teaching literacy, maths, history, art and many other curricular areas. That adds up to a broad range of knowledge, and nobody can specialise in all of it.

What can be seen, then, is that there is a general trend towards increasing specialisation by teachers which correlates with the age ranges taught. However, there is another side to the coin of this apparent disadvantage: your breadth of knowledge brings a perspective that is likely to be near-unique among researchers in your field. How many other medieval historians are also regularly teaching and reading about 20th century politics, for example? How many researchers in social psychology are also regularly teaching both cognitive and biological psychology? Your generalist background can therefore be a strength—it provides a working familiarity with a wide range of scholarship, helping you to find links which might be hard for a more narrowly-focused peer to spot.

In addition, you, as a teacher, have relative freedom about which area to research. You have had time to explore the subject and find the areas that interest you most. This is where you can find your niche—and being based on interests and relevance to your role rather than necessity, it can be highly motivating. In contrast, many university academics chose their field at a relatively young age because they did a PhD in it, often inheriting a supervisor's speciality. They are also subject to intense scrutiny of their research output and their ability to attract grant funding—motivating in its own way, but constraining in terms of what can be investigated and when.

Knowing your subject

How deep is your knowledge? Clearly, to become an expert in your field will take a certain amount of work and specialist reading that will be challenging at first. However, this kind of subject-based research may be less daunting than delving into education research. After all, this is where your background knowledge is already strong.

Additionally, for many teachers, learning more about your own field is very enjoyable. One of the main motivations behind being in the classroom at all is a desire to share fascinating areas of interest with young learners. Frankly, who wouldn't want to help pupils to explore wonderful literature, to understand the joys of science and social science or the intrigue of mathematics, or to develop the gift of speaking a new language . . . the list goes on.

But can you take this to the next level—contribute to real scholarship in your subject, publish and be recognised as a leading voice on certain topics? There are obvious challenges. Despite your relative expertise, there are university-based specialists who have more recent experience, with access to conferences and journals which are hard for you to reach (though see Chapter 3), and are more fully immersed in the scholarly community.

But there is certainly no rule saying that a researcher has to be university-based, or that a school teacher cannot be a researcher. Consider the following:

- Some of the great scholars of the past have been school teachers, including physicist Albert Einstein and educationalist Maria Montessori, while others have worked as medical doctors or in other professions. Apple co-founder Steve Wozniak taught computing, and civil rights leader and author Frederick Douglass was also a teacher. You don't need to be a university academic to make a difference.

- When you completed your undergraduate degree, you were working at a level where your research was fit for publication, or at least not far off. This can be said with confidence because some under-graduates do publish their research—for example, a study based around their final dissertation.

● Even if you have none of the above advantages, you have a sound foundational knowledge in the field and this can be built on. It's easy to underestimate how much more you know about your subject than others do; psychologists call this metacognitive effect the 'curse of knowledge': it's hard to fully recognise our own expertise. What's more, as a teacher your depth of knowledge is likely to have increased significantly since graduation. You have simply had more time to explore the subject. And as most teachers know, explaining things to others is one of the best ways to learn.[1]

● Teachers can and do engage in Masters- or doctoral-level studies alongside their teaching careers, potentially elevating their expertise and putting them in touch with other current experts in the field. Combining studying with a full-time job is challenging, but may lead to career opportunities.

From the research

Key issue: is the gaining of expertise in a subject simply a matter of accumulating knowledge and skills?

What the research says: there is good evidence that experts don't just know more, but they also think differently. In one study, physics problems were shown to participants who were asked to identify key aspects that different problems had in common, and categorise them. Experts (postgraduate physicists) were likely to identify underlying principles such as the conservation of energy, while relative novices were more likely to fixate on surface features, categorising problems in terms of things like the presence of springs and pulleys.[2]

The expertise reversal effect[3] is the finding that classroom support which is beneficial to novices, such as extra information and diagrams, can actually be detrimental to more advanced students, perhaps because it is an unnecessary distraction. This idea fits well with the constructivist approach to learning, which suggest that a learner's current beliefs and schemas are just as important as the input (in terms of information and experiences) that they receive.

Experts can also use their working memory more efficiently. Classic research into chess players has showed that knowledge of strategy greatly expands the grandmaster's ability to use their visual working memory for chess-related problems,[4] (though in general, their working memory capacity remains exactly the same) while problem solving is likely to be much easier for learners who have already automated the basic component skills.[5]

This has implications for student research; while discovery learning has its uses, beginners require considerably more scaffolding, and therefore free discovery and unstructured research are likely to be of most use to scholars (teachers or pupils) who have already established a deep level of knowledge and understanding.

Links with pedagogy

As discussed so far, a teacher could choose to pursue a research career in a particular subject in its own right, but it's also possible for scholarship in the subject and in its pedagogy to be combined. Perhaps you can find out who is investigating the teaching of your own subject(s), and consider the links between research into education more generally and research into your subject in particular. Again, being school-based provides you with a unique insight in comparison to HE staff, and many will jump at the chance to collaborate with you.

An obvious example of subject-based pedagogical research is the work done on STEM education and on literacy, both of which are highly active fields, in part due to their perceived economic importance. However, when you dig around, there are researchers who are looking at the teaching of specific subjects, too. Somebody will be studying the teaching of Music or PSHE or food science—who is it?

There are numerous research sub-fields within the broader bracket of subject-specific pedagogy, including:

Curriculum

What is taught, and why? As teachers we tend to just accept this as a given, but curriculum decisions and changes are made all of the time, and not necessarily for good reasons. Can you find out about the perceived benefit or rationale for including certain items or topics? How does the difficulty level compare to previous years or to other countries? And how does the senior curriculum (e.g. A-Level in your subject) articulate with what is done at higher education or further education level?

Teaching methodology

What methodologies are most helpful for your subject? In the case of evidence-based teaching practices more generally, how do these apply to your subject, and has this ever actually been tested with a real school class? And what about teaching materials—are there particular types of tasks that are very prevalent, and are they evidence based? Could tasks that have been found to work well in other areas of education be adapted to your subject?

Pupil attitudes

You probably have an initial idea of which topics the pupils like and which are less popular. But is this universal, or does it depend on the way they are taught in your own school? If there are topics that are universally unpopular, why is this the case? Does this malaise extend to university level? Are there gender or social differences? And is there any scholarship which suggests ways of improving the image and profile of this topic, or making it more fun to study? Perhaps you could interview pupils who do enjoy these topics.

Any subject can also be stratified by the age group of the pupils themselves, bringing further subdivisions and combinations to these ideas (the History curriculum for early years, for instance).

Links with other researchers

Research doesn't have to be a solo effort. Indeed, it is often most successful when researchers with different skills but similar interests are able to combine their efforts.

As discussed above, a school-based researcher faces numerous disadvantages but also some advantages, too. Their perspective in educating younger learners in the subject may be something that university-based researchers have little experience of, and they may well be interested in finding out more about the content that is taught in schools. From a university point of view it's valuable to attract new prospective students, meaning that they may also be interested in coming to give talks to your classes (Chapter 16 looks more at how you can build a local area network for research-engaged teachers).

Does this matter to pupils?

The importance of the depth of a teacher's subject knowledge to learner achievement is quite hard to gauge, and the research literature is surprisingly equivocal on the issue.

It might seem obvious that a teacher who knows more about their subject will be able to teach it more effectively due to their depth of understanding, their ability to field a broad range of pupil questions, and a mental storehouse of explanations and examples. However, in comparison to other issues that affect pupil outcomes, John Hattie and colleagues have found that a teacher's subject expertise has a relatively modest effect when measured in terms of pupil outcomes.[6]

There could be other benefits, however. As a more knowledgeable teacher, you will be more confident, and may therefore be more likely to inspire pupils to take the subject or continue with it to further study. Parents and colleagues are also likely to notice and be impressed. There could be opportunities with exam boards and other organisations as your expertise becomes well known, particularly if there are key syllabus areas that you understand better than most of your peers.

In addition, beyond the whole class setting, you will be in a better position to guide individual learning like that of the type described in the case study of pupils and citizen science (see below). This might not make a large difference statistically, but a pupil who is engaging in and with research will have an advantage at university interviews, and will gain a skill set that will help them during a degree.

Finally, it's clearly going to be harmful for pupils if a curious and talented teacher leaves the profession due to boredom or frustration with continually repeating the same lessons. Getting involved in research in your subject can help to keep you more engaged and interested in your career, helping to keep a good teacher in the classroom.

Case study: pupils and citizen science

Citizen science is a form of crowdsourcing of scientific observations which can then be collated and analysed by researchers. For example, this could include asking the public to report sightings of migratory birds in order to keep track of changes to the populations of these species, environmental agencies providing equipment in order for the public to record levels of air pollution, or astronomy organisations asking members of the public to analyse small data sets, selected from the readings made by satellites.

In the following case, school pupils teamed up with their research-engaged teacher to investigate the way that classroom layout affects pupil engagement:

Aqsa is a Biology teacher who is engaged in a programme of research about classroom management. She is interested in how the layout of classrooms can influence pupil behaviour, and decided to observe for signs of stress. With the permission of school management and with colleagues having been made aware, she worked together with pupils who were studying a Biology module to make up a suitable observation schedule.

While there are many possible behavioural signs of stress, the research team chose to focus on nail-biting as an easily-observed and reasonably objective sign. Aqsa and her pupils reasoned that this would be relatively easy to spot, even while learners were engaged in classwork. They also reasoned that while pupils could bite their nails for lots of reasons, it was more likely to happen in a stressful environment.

Her pupils then acted as research assistants during their other lessons. To avoid any intrusion or embarrassment on behalf of her colleagues, no teacher or subject names were recorded on the observation schedule—pupils simply circled the classroom layout that most resembled the room their were in at the time of the observation from a selection of diagrams (showing horseshoe, clusters of desks, rows, individual desks, etc) and then made an estimate of the percentage of classmates who had engaged in nail-biting during the lesson. Over the course of three weeks, several hundred of these observation schedules were completed.

As can be seen from this example, pupils can work together with a teacher in order to gather data. In this example, the teacher follows the example of citizen science in gathering large amounts of observational data. What differs is that the observers were involved in the research design as well as the data gathering.

In many ways, the study showed an ingenious design, with its light-touch observation of classroom layout and signs of stress. What it sacrifices in terms of accuracy and sensitivity of the measurements it makes up for in terms of gaining large amounts of data, which may show useful trends.

However, it could be argued that even the limited amount of observation that pupils were engaged in during this study could occupy their working memory capacity and therefore distract them from what they should have been focusing on in class. A preferable alternative would be to base this sort of study in a different context, such as during extra-curricular activities or corridor behaviour.

Pupil research projects

So far this chapter has focused mainly on subject-based research engagement for teachers, but as mentioned earlier, our pupils also engage in research at various times during school. Research is built into the curriculum, both as a means of learning and consolidating topic content, and to learn research skills which will be of use in the future.

In science, such research often takes the form of classroom demonstrations and experiments. While most are nothing groundbreaking and are often deliberately based around demonstrations of classic findings, there are a few cases where school pupils have made and even published novel scientific discoveries.

In other subjects, research plays an important role too. In social sciences such as History, this is often based around investigating and synthesising sources. As pupils get older they will increasingly tackle optional texts, and begin to explore their school subjects more independently.

Some pupils may choose to conduct independent research projects outside of the requirements of their school subjects. Such learners are often highly motivated, pursuing something unique because of their intrinsic curiosity. As a result, their projects can be highly impressive to universities and employers if mentioned in UCAS applications or discussed at interviews.

Impetus for a student project

The motivation to conduct research outside of school courses can have various sources. Perhaps a pupil can combine a personal interest with their subject in some way. For example, a pupil who enjoys coding might engage well with designing an online research task for their subject, while one who plays tennis might like to investigate evidence-based ways of increasing the power of a serve or improving stamina. There may also be cases where one or more pupils want to collaborate—perhaps to find out more about an area of study which they both enjoyed.

A further possibility is that the teacher may take the lead on a project, recruiting pupils in a kind of research assistant role, in a similar way to how a lead researcher at university may assemble a team of junior academics and postgraduate students.

The common theme for all of these ideas is that they are pursued for their own sake, driven by curiosity and a desire to find out something new. The fundamental skills gained through conducting research are likely to be similar to those within a school course, but the motivation is likely to be more lasting. It is based on an autonomous choice, a sense of purpose and competence in the area at hand, and (perhaps) a social aspect too—the key aspects of motivation according to self-determination theory.[7]

There may also be different end results. If pupils are not conducting research to increase their chances of a top grade, then why are they doing so? Some schools may offer prizes or other recognition awards for independent scholarship. And there is the possibility of broader rewards outside of the school itself: publication, conference presentations, articles in newspapers . . .or the beginning of an academic CV.

Guiding student research

Many pupils will already have a rudimentary set of research skills, as these are integral to their schoolwork. Their existing strengths may include:

- Using the library and finding sources.
- Searching online.
- Skim reading texts.
- Mathematical calculations.
- Drawing up graphs.
- Writing a bibliography or references in a standard format.

However, like any novice researcher, pupils can benefit from guidance. For this reason, schools which have a programme supporting student research may choose to allocate staff as supervisors. This is, of course, the model operated for university research students.

If this is the approach followed by you or your school, you may find yourself in the mentor role, guiding others as they move through some of the processes described in this book. Doing so is a useful learning experience for both parties, and also helps to prepare you for future mentoring or coaching of research-engaged colleagues, if you ever find yourself in a research lead role (see next chapter).

Research project: a useful research project could look at the expertise of various teachers, and/or their attitudes to developing their expertise. Do they see themselves as subject experts, and how much do they value opportunities to advance their expertise in particular areas of their teaching subject(s)? A working hypothesis could be that teachers who value and/or try to develop their expertise also experience higher levels of well-being.

How to do it: teachers' beliefs and the value they place on professional learning could be investigated via semi-structured interviews (see Chapter 12). For a more developed project, why not compare this to subjective well-being? One good way of making such a measure is to use a standardised questionnaire such as the Oxford Happiness Scale.[8] The limitation of that particular methodology is that it relies on a 'snapshot' self-report, which could be biased both by current mood and/or by the accuracy of participants' memories, and you may therefore ask people to track their sense of well-being over a period of time.

In terms of background research, it would be useful to search for studies with 'professional identity' as a keyword, and consider drawing parallels with findings from other careers.

Concluding comments

Educational research is not the only type of research that is relevant to the teacher. Many research-engaged teachers instead develop their practice and increase research engagement by engaging further with research in their own subject. Although we face barriers to this, we are also—as we have seen—in a position of strength in terms of our breadth of knowledge.

The scholarship around how our teaching subject is delivered is another area that can be of interest, and teachers again have advantages over HE staff due to their practical experience and everyday access to younger learners. For some, this will culminate in sharing and publishing their scholarship—processes explained in the final chapter of this book.

Research can play a valuable and motivating role in pupils' learning too, but it requires a set of skills with a steep learning curve. By taking a research mentor role, the research-engaged teacher can manage those demands, taking the lead on issues such as ethics, research design and data analysis, while still allowing pupils to engage with ideas autonomously and fuel their own curiosity.

Further reading

'Unleashing great teaching' by David Weston and Bridget Clay (2018, Routledge) usefully delves into what successful teacher professional learning is all about, and how best to do it.

There are numerous books aimed at guiding student research projects, or at integrating project-based learning into teaching. Ross Cooper and Erin Murphy's 'Hacking project based learning: 10 easy steps to PBL and inquiry in the classroom' (2016, Times 10 Publishing) is a fun and accessible example.

Discussion questions

- At what level is your own subject expertise?
- Do you know any researchers who investigate the pedagogy of your subject specialism, and if not, could you find out about some and make contact?

- What practical issues would you have to consider when guiding a pupil's independent research?
- Can a school pupil make a novel scientific discovery?

Notes

1 Koh, A. W. L., Lee, S. C., and Lim, S. W. H. (2018). The learning benefits of teaching: A retrieval practice hypothesis. *Applied Cognitive Psychology*, 32(3), 401–410.
2 Chi, M. T. H., Glaser, R., and Rees, E. (1982). Expertise in problem solving. In R. S. Sternberg (Ed.). *Advances in the psychology of human intelligence*, Vol. 1 (pp. 1–75). Hillsdale, NJ: Erlbaum.
3 Kalyuga, S. (2007). Expertise reversal effect and its implications for learner-tailored instruction. *Educational Psychology Review*, 19(4), 509–539.
4 Chase, W. G, and Simon, H. A. (1973). The mind's eye in chess. In W. G. Chase (Ed.), *Visual information processing* (pp. 215–281). New York: Academic Press.
5 Sweller, J., and Chandler, P. (1991). Evidence for cognitive load theory. *Cognition and Instruction*, 8(4), 351–362.
6 Hattie, J. (2008). *Visible learning: A synthesis of over 800 meta-analyses relating to achievement.* London: Routledge.
7 Ryan, R. M., and Deci, E. L. (2017). *Self-determination theory: Basic psychological needs in motivation, development, and wellness.* London: Guilford Publications.
8 http://www.happiness-survey.com/

PART 3

The networked teacher-researcher

The previous part of this book has explored the practicalities of making research activities a part of your ongoing professional practice. Rejecting the idea that we should 'leave it to the experts', the foregoing chapters have worked through the skills and knowledge that a teacher needs in order to start conducting ethical, valid and worthwhile research and to analyse their own findings. It has been argued that in order to gain findings that are worth sharing and acting upon, we need to ensure that our own research processes are as bias-free as possible, and that we understand how variables and data analysis work.

The final part of this book looks at how we can site this research process within a broader educational context, and draw on the support of others. After all, no teacher is an island! How can the research-engaged teacher gain support from their colleagues or from peers in other organisations, share ideas and disseminate the outcome of their own research work with the broader community?

 # The 'research lead' role

Many schools are looking at giving one or more teachers the responsibility for disseminating research among staff. This chapter looks at how to play this role effectively.

In some cases, you may have (or have plans to obtain) an official 'research lead' role. Perhaps you are a deputy headteacher in charge of research, or are heading up a school research centre, and have become the de facto research lead for projects carried out under its auspices.

Alternatively, this may be more of an informal position—you have become known as the 'go to' person for research issues. Perhaps you are one of the most prominent research-engaged teachers in the school, and find yourself, in effect, as a research champion. This could mean that people come to you with practical questions about the methodology of their own research. You may also find yourself having to field queries or emails about the research literature, such as 'what's the latest evidence on spacing?', or 'has anyone tried retrieval practice with Year 8 music pupils?', or 'is it true that technique Z has been debunked?'. This chapter aims to equip you for such tasks.

What is the purpose of a research lead?

There are many people in any school staff who are more than just a teacher—some also coach a sports team, act as school counsellor or edit the school newspaper. You, in addition to your teaching and any other roles, are taking the lead on research in school.

Philosophically, what is a research lead actually for, and is having such a role even a good idea? As government advisor and prolific behaviour blogger Tom Bennett said in 2017, "The Research Lead can connect the school to the greater world of education research, while simultaneously acting as filter. The Lead can convert the school from an island, to an archipelago, to a peninsula, and be a powerful agent of change".[1]

Bennett suggests several possible variants of the role:

- The gatekeeper—a conduit for research in general.
- The devil's advocate—a 'critical friend' who will challenge staff on their practices.
- The project manager—tasked with pushing forward a particular change, finding out about it and how it has been done elsewhere.
- The consigliere—a special advisor to management, rather than to the staff as a whole.

There are other possible models, too, and many leads may assume a fusion of the versions listed. More broadly they function as a link between the teachers and the people who are producing research.

Some may wonder whether duties such as keeping teaching and learning approaches up-to-date should more properly be the responsibility of school management. It could also be said that having a single person in charge of disseminating research to other teachers could be limiting, and from that point of view it is worth balancing out the potential benefits (efficiency; greater expertise of the person in the lead role meaning that more suitable research is found) against the potential drawbacks (other teachers may feel less engaged without autonomy over their research activities; less knock-on benefit to their research skills).

Rather than seeing the research lead as being a conduit for getting research information to the staff, it could help to see them as a 'first among equals'—a role model and leader, helping others to engage with research rather than doing it for them.

The research lead will also play a key role in accessing and sharing information. Like a school librarian, they can use their specialised skills to support other members of staff. This doesn't mean that other staff are never accessing information themselves—merely that someone with more expertise can point the way and assist where necessary.

In such a role, the research lead could potentially do some or all of the following:

- Summarise and share relevant new journal articles.
- Summarise/comment on and share new reports released by government bodies or education organisations such as EEF.
- Organise in-school research conferences.
- Organise visiting speakers and research-based professional learning sessions.
- Organise staff research reading groups or discussion forums.
- Manage resources in school, such as library support, IT facilities and research space.
- Provide or arrange 1-to-1 coaching of staff as they engage in research projects.
- Identify appropriate external courses for staff to engage in, and support them during such courses.
- Ensure that staff members' research outputs are disseminated, for example in school newsletters and on display boards.
- Form links with other schools.
- Liaise with ethics bodies e.g. at local authority or HE level.
- Liaise with teacher education/ITT organisations.
- Advocate for the importance of research in education.
- Share any of the above work on social media.

Some leads may also support early-career teachers, and have direct input into a school-wide professional learning programme.

From the research

Key issue: what prompts people to change their habits and behaviour? As a research lead, you may find yourself advocating for research amid a climate of scepticism. 'Why do I need to read research', some may ask, 'when I already know how to teach?'

What the research says: theories of personality suggest that change is actually quite difficult, as people tend to retain the same traits—extraversion, neuroticism, etc—for their whole lifespan. But there are areas of research that can be applied.

Behaviourist theory suggests that change is achieved via rewards and punishments, with rewards (i.e. good/pleasant outcomes) causing behaviour to increase or strengthen. However, this instrumental approach is often seen as over-simplistic when applied to real human behaviour (much of the foundational research was done on animals), and rewards can even demotivate over a longer timespan (see Chapter 15).

An alternative which is growing in popularity is **nudge psychology**, whereby behaviour change is motivated by making a task easier or more attractive to do—a small nudge in the right direction, rather than a big reward or threat. Examples include personalising a message (such as using a 1-to-1 message asking a colleague to do something, rather than a blanket announcement), or reducing psychological friction by making a task easier to access. A specific example could be equipping a 'teacher research room' with excellent IT facilities, free coffee and locating it immediately opposite the staff room so that people walk past it every day. Leaving a research book (like this one) on a table in the staffroom, rather than in the school library, would be another simple nudge. Asking teachers to state an explicit professional learning goal can also be a form of nudge, drawing on their sense of social commitment. None of these things require rewards or punishments.

Social psychologists have increasingly focused on the role of identity in behaviour change. A person's **social identity** is how they define themselves in terms of the social group(s) that they are a member of, such as being a teacher or a researcher (or both). When people identify with a group, they are motivated to make the group successful, and will even accept a situation that makes them worse off if it means that their group is seen in a better light than other groups.[2]

One way to achieve this with teachers is to encourage seeing research as being part of their role (and not someone else's job) by using inclusive messages that tie in to their existing values. Social psychology research has shown that simply using language that makes a shared identity more salient can change people's behaviour.[3] For example, consider a message that begins, 'As professionals who care about ensuring that our teaching is effective, we . . .'. Such a message is appealing to a shared group 'we', and encouraging anyone who cares about effective teaching (i.e. most teachers) to identify with that group. Such phrasing is more persuasive than messages which state 'you should do x', as behaviour change based on identity is stronger and more lasting than that which is motivated by guilt or obligation.

Professional expertise

It is likely to be teachers who are already research engaged that are attracted to a research lead role. If you are (or intend to be) a lead, perhaps you have already conducted some research of your own, and have a good understanding of the various issues discussed earlier in this book. Many research leads already have a Masters or a doctoral degree in education. There is a lot to be said for personal experience combined with enthusiasm—but at the same time, none of us know everything about research, and any research lead should consider new (or weaker) areas of professional knowledge and skill that they could develop.

To start with, there are many different types of research methodology. Could you expand your own expertise, and learn more about the many options ranging from randomised controlled trials to naturalistic observations of discourse? If you are mainly focused on education research, you may also find it helpful to consider how colleagues in the various subject departments (or from different academic backgrounds) conceptualise research. For some, research may be seen as mainly a matter of reading and analysis, and not as data gathering. Others may see it only in terms of the results of experiments, and may need encouraged to consider other types of evidence. Understanding how research works in the various subjects will help in identifying the starting point from which any training can begin.

Some universities and other organisations offer specific short courses in particular methodologies. For example, it is possible to do courses just on systematic reviews, and having such a qualification will increase your chances of getting a review pre-registered with an organisation such as PROSPERO, should you choose to publish your work.

Other areas where it could be valuable to engage in professional learning via courses or workshops include:

- Academic writing.
- Time management and event planning.
- Preparing grant proposals.
- Statistics.

Case study: the research lead

Consider the following case of a school deputy headteacher who is highly research engaged. She plays the role of an informal research lead, setting up staff discussion groups and sharing new evidence-informed ideas:

> Clare is a teacher of Biology and Psychology, a teacher-researcher and a blogger. She is the deputy head of an all-through school in Northern Ireland. She is also a well-known and effective speaker, often invited to education conferences at which she makes contacts with some of the biggest names in education and educational psychology.

Some of these people later visit the school as a favour to Clare, and speak to the staff about their work.

Due to her own educational background, Clare is particularly attracted to studies based on cutting-edge neuroscience. For example, she finds herself fascinated by research which looks at brain function in pupils with dyslexia or dyscalculia, as well as the long-term neurological effects of neglectful parenting. She receives email updates on such studies from several journals, and summarises them for her colleagues. Staff in the primary school have shown a particular interest in this support.

Clare has also prepared a list of '10 evidence-based teaching habits', loosely based on the conclusions of a book about applying psychology in the classroom.

This example shows both the strengths and weaknesses of a research lead role, particularly one which develops organically. Clare shares research summaries with staff and these are appreciated, but this arrangement does appear rather one-way, with little in the way of negotiating priorities collectively. An alternative might be to share a wider range of articles as titles only, and ask the staff themselves which ones they would like to have summarised.

Clare is clearly an impressive and research-engaged professional and an asset to her school, not least via her impressive contacts. Her remit seems quite vague and narrow, though, and speaks to the benefits of the research lead role being specified (and perhaps of separating it from management duties). Her choice of evidence-based strategies for the staff takes a top-down approach (rather like the case study in Chapter 5); it might be more motivating and democratic to recommend the book as the focus for a staff research reading group, and then to seek departmental feedback on what they would most like to explore further.

Fielding research queries

As already noted, the research lead often finds themselves in a position of fielding queries and supporting others in their learning and research. In this sense, the role may have similar challenges to that of the research supervisor at university level; in some cases, the supervisee will have better up-to-date technical knowledge on the specific research literature, but the supervisor still needs to use their experience and skills to guide the process.

You may also have other people that you rely on for information about specific areas, and this can include the community of teacher-researchers in the school, as well as outside experts. As an analogy, consider the role of a sports team manager—they have a lot of technical knowledge, but they often have colleagues with more specific remits (e.g. a fitness coach or a dietary expert). In short, they don't try to know everything about all areas.

Specific considerations when dealing with research-based queries include:

- Allocate time to reading questions and to responding. Manage expectations—teachers shouldn't expect an immediate response.

- If a query is particularly complex, ask teachers to schedule a meeting. You could allocate particular times of the week to this task, or set up an online appointment system.

- Read up on the teacher's chosen area of research, but don't put pressure yourself to become an expert on it. Ideally, they should be doing the work by writing a literature review for themselves.

- If you are uncertain, say so. You could tentatively suggest a possible solution, and ask the teacher themselves to find out more.

- If the teacher is still at an early stage, they may need to be pointed in the direction of major theories and researchers in their chosen area. If you are unsure about these in a specific field of education, draw on your network of contacts for suggestions, or suggest that the teacher does so via a local network or online.

Overall, when it comes to guiding other teachers' research, you will find yourself navigating between the role of expert and a more generic leadership role. You may at times find yourself reflecting questions back to the teacher—a popular technique in coaching. For example, if asked what is the best sample size to use for a research study, you could respond with something like 'what do *you* think the best sample size would be?', rather than trying to answer the question more directly.[4] If the teacher in question is really unsure, it may be best to ask them to go back and read some more.

With experience, and as time goes on, you will find yourself increasingly comfortable at guiding the research process.

Research project: a key role of a research lead (or a member of staff who plays that role informally) is to review and summarise research. Therefore, this chapter's project will involve preparing a literature review—a form of research output in its own right, but not one that involves gathering new data. A review will be useful for colleagues, and could later form the basis of an article, Masters dissertation or the introduction chapter for a doctorate.

How to do it: there are no absolutes in terms of how detailed a literature review should be, or how long. However, it should generally be quite narrow in scope—the idea is to review all of the studies on a particular area, and therefore depth rather than breadth is what you are aiming for.

A good starting point would be to cover ten or twelve studies, most of them recent and all on very closely related issue. Any topic could be covered—it would probably make sense to try to identify a topic that fits with school or national priorities, or which is of particular concern to you or to other teachers in your school. Examples might include formative assessment in science, strategies for effective secondary school homework, motivation in personal reading, the use of listening practice in the modern languages classroom . . . the list goes on.

For a good published example, refer to the review on 'learning versus performance' by Nick Soderstrom and Robert Bjork.[5]

(continued)

(continued)

This begins with a general introduction, and then divides the topic up by aspects and types of studies, such as 'verbal learning'. Each study is summarised, and each sub-section is followed by an interim summary as well.

Concluding comments

Some people have their concerns about the research lead role. It could, in some circumstances, lead to teachers thinking 'that's not my job', and engaging with research less than they otherwise would. This problem could be exacerbated if the format of the engagement with their school lead is very passive (simply receiving information).

However, this chapter has described how a research lead can be a leader among equals and an agent of change. They can advocate for the work of their colleagues and help to bring it to a wider audience. They can provide expert technical support in the background, supporting rather than undermining other teachers' ability to find information. And they can play a research supervisor role, fielding queries and exploring interesting new areas in tandem with colleagues or school research teams.

The next chapter discusses how a research-engaged teacher or lead can help to build a culture of research throughout the school; it naturally links with and follows on from this one.

Further reading

As mentioned earlier in this chapter, Tom Bennett discusses the research lead role, and how it can provide a useful conduit, unlocking research for the staff as a whole. His chapter is part of the book 'Flip the System UK: A Teachers' Manifesto' edited by Rycroft-Smith & Dutaut (2017, Routledge).

As a research lead, one of the best starting points for information is the work of the Educational Endowment Foundation (EEF), whose toolkit may be best shared in full or could be summarised. There are also separate reports on specific issues; the 2018 review of metacognition[6] is an excellent example.

It is wise to sign up to email alerts from education-related journals. Some websites and blogs also summarise recent findings.

Discussion questions

◉ What qualities are required in a good research lead?

◉ What advantages and drawbacks might there be to the research lead role, compared with having individual teachers accessing research directly?

◉ Is it beneficial for the research lead to be a member of school management?

◉ What external links/partnerships might help a research lead to do an effective job?

Notes

1 Bennett, T. (2017). There are no ninjas: Why the research revolution might rescue teaching. In L. Rycroft-Smith and J. L. Dutaut (Eds.), *Flip the system UK: A teachers' manifesto* (pp. 7–14) (p. 9). Abingdon, UK: Routledge.
2 Tajfel, H., and Turner, J. C. (1979). An integrative theory of intergroup conflict. In M. J. Hatch and M. Schultz (Eds.), *Organizational identity: A reader* (pp. 56–65). Oxford: Oxford University Press.
3 Levine, M., Prosser, A., Evans, D., and Reicher, S. (2005). Identity and emergency intervention: How social group membership and inclusiveness of group boundaries shape helping behavior. *Personality and Social Psychology Bulletin*, 31(4), 443–453.
4 Although you could also guide them to look into running a power analysis— a method of calculating how many participants will be needed in order to statistically detect a given effect size.
5 Soderstrom, N. C., and Bjork, R. A. (2015). Learning versus performance: An integrative review. *Perspectives on Psychological Science*, 10(2), 176–199.
6 https://educationendowmentfoundation.org.uk/tools/guidance-reports/ metacognition-and-self-regulated-learning/

A school culture of research

The research lead, discussed in the previous chapter, represents the beginning of a process of establishing research engagement as a norm throughout the school. A proactive teacher-researcher can accomplish a lot on their own, but there can be little doubt that building a school-wide network can amplify the effects. A broader support system can help you find the resources you need and fill any knowledge gaps that you might have, allowing you to specialise in what you do best. It can also support you in developing new skills, thus preparing you for a greater impact over the long term.

The largest-scale iteration of such systems would be for an entire school culture of research and enquiry, such as being a designated 'research school' or developing a school-based research centre or institute, and that option is a focus of the current chapter. We will also consider how, in the absence of such a structure, you can build an effective peer network, whether you are working as a research lead or simply as a research-engaged teacher acting independently.

Preparing the ground

To use a gardening analogy, it's difficult to grow anything without preparing the ground first. In the case of building a research culture in your school and beyond, it's important that fellow professionals on the staff are at least interested in research. It therefore makes sense to stimulate or nurture that interest prior to asking them to make use of or otherwise engage in research. Without doing so, sharing your ideas or your own work will be a lot more difficult, as others will be less receptive to it—and perhaps even openly hostile.

On the positive side, you may well be pushing at an open door. Many teachers already have a background and interest in research, and will appreciate its value. Such teachers may have more technical concerns—how do we make the research valid, or ensure that it is ethical? Isn't this best done by people with specific training? You are now well equipped to deal with these concerns.

One possible starting point would be to share a questionnaire asking about teachers' experiences with research, and asking them to express their thoughts on how it could become a more valuable part of their career (this is the project outlined at the end of Chapter 11). This can help you to find out how much people know, and roughly gauge the proportion of staff willing to:

- Use research more to inform their practice.
- Carry out or collaborate on practical educational research projects.
- Engage in scholarship in their own teaching subject.

Certainly, this may show that many people on the staff think that research is just not for them. But more importantly, you will have found out who is interested in adopting certain changes, and what kind of support they might need. It would be a good idea to ask participants to state their identity (voluntarily, and with the usual confidentiality of findings assured), so that you could contact them with further opportunities.

In order to further raise interest and awareness, you could consider sharing your own experiences that have led you to this point, perhaps as a short talk to the whole staff. Highlighting some of your early mistakes and misconceptions can be embarrassing, but will help to make the whole process seem more accessible. It would also be helpful to distribute materials such as one of the early chapters of this book, or other publications that explain the value of research to a teacher's professionalism.

Finding out who on the staff is already research engaged may lead to some surprises. It is certainly useful to find out who might be willing to become so if certain barriers were removed. It may be the case that many people are already aware of the value of research, but have not fully thought through all of the implications this has for their practice. And perhaps they don't regularly discuss these interests with colleagues. The aim, then, will be to help the school move from having a group of interested individuals to having a whole-school culture where research is welcomed, encouraged and supported.

Reading and sharing

A natural next step would be to establish a research reading group. Like any book group, this could involve a book being selected every month (perhaps with each member of the group adding a new choice to the list), with follow-up meetings where the main issues and themes are discussed.

An alternative model—which would work well with the calendar and the workload associated with schools—would be to have more frequent meetings (once a week, perhaps) and shorter items to read. Research papers of a dozen pages or less would be suitable choices, as would chapters from books, or research summaries (see Chapter 3 for more on research sources). Blog posts and policy documents could also be included for variety.

Holding regular meetings brings certain advantages which are already familiar to book group enthusiasts—it provides a sociable and supportive atmosphere, and allows reading to be explored in a level of depth that is only possible when more than one person has the details fresh in their mind (very different from just telling a colleague about something that you have read!).

There are also ways of leveraging this learning to even better effect, for example:

- Establishing a Twitter hashtag for use in-between group meetings, allowing for debate with a broader group of teachers, and perhaps even with the book authors.[1]

- Asking members to take turns to summarise a text at a staff meeting.
- Establishing a teaching & learning blog, in which the most useful new ideas can be shared more widely and with supporting details (perhaps with two or more teachers presenting their individual takes on the issue).
- Reviewing books or articles for a school magazine.

It is often suggested that around 6–10 people is the optimal size for a book group. For that reason, there will (hopefully—at least in typically sized schools) be the potential to have more than one group running as time goes on. These could focus on subject areas (science teachers, social science, etc), different topic interests (cognitive psychology, well-being, etc), or remain more mixed.

A research centre

When a culture of research has been established and there is a sizeable group of staff who are beginning to engage with research, it might make sense to formalise this group in some way. Some schools have established a **school research centre**—a semi-autonomous unit or department within the school which has responsibility for overseeing, supporting and planning research activities.

Case study: a school research centre

What is involved in establishing a teacher research centre? What are the challenges, and what type of activity might take place on a day-to-day basis? The following case describes how a large secondary school undertook this process:

> A group of research-engaged teachers had the idea to launch a research centre in their school. They began with two aims

(continued)

(continued)

in particular: to build a culture of research throughout the school, and to improve communication about research between staff, pupils and the wider community.

The first stage was largely organisational. In a series of meetings, the founding teachers agreed with management that they would establish a research board which would have oversight of research activities throughout the school. This board would establish a system for proposing new projects, as well as putting an ethics procedure in place to scrutinise proposals and consider any impact on pupil well-being.

Via a call for volunteers, the board was established with two members of management and five from among the teaching and pastoral staff. One of the teachers who had proposed the centre agreed to act as its director.

There was an initial flurry of interest as staff proposed projects, and it became clear to the board that many teachers would require guidance in terms of the scope and methodology of their research. After a proposal had been considered, the proposer was offered a research mentor, and the board worked to help them establish links with external researchers, too.

As time went on, though, it became clear that there were some tensions and disagreement about how to run the centre. Some staff felt that it should only focus on educational research, while others saw its remit as being broader, including subject-based scholarship. Each teacher's proposal had to be approved by their head of department, and this led to delays. There were also disagreements about how strict the centre should be on ethical and methodological issues, with some board members voicing concerns that they shouldn't discourage enthusiastic teachers with pedantic objections. The research centre also lacked a defined space, being in essence a virtual centre, with little day-to-day communication among the staff involved. The regularity of board meetings dwindled, and the school's more research-engaged teachers began to see the entire process as burdensome and bureaucratic.

This case explains a promising example of a research centre, but one which experienced flaws in implementation and ultimately lost momentum.

Part of the problem may have resulted from tensions between different priorities within the school—teachers who wanted to develop their research engagement for a variety of reasons, and promoted staff who didn't see it as a priority but rather as something to be managed. The school appear to have wanted the research centre to exist, but been unwilling to relinquish real control to it.

It's also notable that the process was quite passive. Rather than setting a research agenda, the centre waited for teachers to propose ideas, which were then processed. It may have been better to work from a democratically agreed research agenda or policy, or to ask each department to set a particular priority. This would have given the centre a more motivating, grass-roots approach and avoided conflicts between the teachers and their line managers.

Promoting teacher buy-in

What would a successful school research centre or support process look like? As the school research centre case study shows, it shouldn't just be a filtering system, approving some research proposals and rejecting others, as doing so can lead to teachers lacking an incentive to engage. A key question is to ask why a research-engaged member of staff would want to be part of the centre or school-wide movement at all? What is going to make them buy in to the school's process, rather than working more autonomously?

If a community is to be built then this issue needs to be considered and tackled. Overall, for a teacher to engage, there needs to be more for them to gain than there is for them to lose. Some important points include:

- The process needs to be quick. Long delays—perhaps associated with infrequent meetings of the senior staff responsible, with bureaucratic systems, or with research activities being seen as low priority, could lead to teachers becoming frustrated.

- A high success rate is helpful. Why give people little or no guidance on ethics and methodology, and then reject their research proposals? A more proactive approach could be to run CPD workshops where staff draft up proposals, with submission to the next level being an option thereafter.

- According to the principles of nudge psychology (see previous chapter), the process needs to be as low friction as possible. This could mean making the initial proposal quick and easy to do, building in time for research activities (e.g. in lieu of other school duties), and setting up personalised reminders and emails to prompt staff.

- Some kind of social recognition could be built in to the process. This could include having a dedicated research space for teachers who are engaged in research projects, or allocating them university library access. Even just the status of labelling staff as 'teacher-researcher' on staff lists or on a display board in school (perhaps with a brief summary of their current project) could be motivating, and encourage them to see research as part of their professional identity.

Overall, there are many barriers to engaging with research (see Chapter 2) and a research centre should help to overcome these, rather than adding to them.

From the research

Key issue: what is the best way to build a community of practitioners who are all enthusiastically engaged with research?

What the research says: the idea of a learning community has been considered in multiple educational contexts. Jean Lave and Etienne Wenger have described an authentic and self-sustaining group of learners as a 'community of practice'. Based on anthropological studies of how people learn traditional skills via apprenticeship, their view sees learning as a social craft rather than an individual cognitive process.

In such a context, mastery of a skill can arrive without direct teaching. As Lave puts it, "developing an identity as a member of a community and becoming highly skilful are part of the same process, with the former motivating, shaping, and giving meaning to the latter".[2]

In such a context, learning can be thought of as a more fluid process than is the case with traditional CPD. For a successful community of practice to develop, knowledge must be openly accessible to all (rather than controlled), and people must be allowed to gradually become central members of the community in the course of everyday activities (rather than as the result of direct teaching) having previously been on the periphery.

Monitoring and encouragement

It is no doubt tempting for management staff to keep track of teachers' research activities. However, is this necessary, or even helpful? Judyth Sachs discusses the creeping managerialism in schools worldwide, noting that "Performance cultures within public service organizations imply a low level of trust in the professionalism of their employees",[3] and furthermore arguing that this situation serves to reduce rather than boost professionalism over the long term. Management checks on what teacher-researchers are doing are therefore likely to have little benefit, while adding to workload. Such top-down oversight may result in teachers engaging with research in a half-hearted way because it's expected, and not because it has become part of their professional identity.

It is also tempting to ask how we should reward teachers' engagement with school research activities. After all, they are doing extra work—don't they deserve something back? However, it's worth being cautious about offering incentives. Research into motivation suggests that rewards can actually be counterproductive, reducing effort and motivation because people perceive them as reducing choice and control.[4] This can reduce engagement and persistence in future.

Instead, some of the strongest motivators are a sense of freedom and of belonging to a community. These lead to lasting, intrinsic motivation, where people begin a task quickly, work on it intensely and are not easily discouraged.

In addition, research activities should not be taking teachers significantly beyond their core hours, due to the risk of overwork and burnout. If schools were to pay staff extra for research work, for example, these tasks would essentially turn into a part-time job on top of their main role. It would be better to think about how other duties could make way, to allow a teacher to engage with research as part of their core responsibilities.

In those schools who have a research lead, this is typically a promoted post. Other teachers who have significant research responsibilities or lead teams of teacher-researchers could reasonably be seen as working at an equivalent level to senior teachers or heads of departments, with an impact either on pay or contact hours. Teacher-researchers could be given a percentage of time off timetable for the duration of their project, or given the opportunity to access small research grants (one purpose of such grants might be to pay for staffing to cover any reduced class contact time). Additionally, as mentioned earlier (see the case study on p. 217). there could be more subtle payoffs in terms of status or privileges.

Overall, teachers need to feel that they are engaging with research through choice and because they want to be part of a social community, not because they are forced to. Frustrating though it may be when some teachers refuse to engage, making the process mandatory is not a good way of motivating participation, and is unlikely to be sustainable.

Research project: a project which could be valuable to your classroom and which could also help you to understand how best to establish and run a research centre would be to investigate the processes involved in carrying out a project. This could focus on motivation, planning, organisation or the importance of social support. Focusing on planning, for example, you could investigate how accurate and realistic people's research plans are, and what action they take to deal with problems with their initial plan. The **planning fallacy** is the psychological finding that people tend to allocate too little time to their plans, even when they have past experience of doing similar tasks, and even when given real examples of other people's timescales.[5]

How to do it: when investigating the running of a project, it would be best if the data were authentic and specific to your context. If you have enough colleagues or other contacts who are currently planning a research project, or if (perhaps as part of a professional learning workshop) every staff member is asked to come up with an initial plan, these plans could form the data for your investigation. Alternatively, you could investigate the planning processes used by pupils in your school. The data will be authentic, and you can still benefit from the ease of analysing quantitative data if you use numerical details such as the amount of time allocated to various parts of the process: background reading, data gathering, writing up, etc.

Drawing on background research into the planning fallacy, you could also run a simple experiment where one group is given example timescales and the other is not, and then measure how much time they think will be needed for their own plan. Alternatively, you could give each participant a brief personality test,[6] to see how personality might interact with the accuracy of planning or the choices made. For example, do extraverts allow more time for supervision meetings? Do people who are more psychologically open to experience also allow more time for background reading? Are neurotic people more pessimistic in their planned timescales? You can aim to see whether there is a correlation (see Chapter 10) between the score on any particular personality characteristic and the amount of time (or percentage of available time) that has been allocated in the plan.

Concluding comments

We are still in the early days of teaching being considered a research-based profession, and there is a tendency for any individual teacher-researcher to feel isolated in their school, fail to fully develop, and in some cases perhaps give up entirely due to the challenges of engaging in the process alone. As has been discussed in this chapter, schools can implement systems which boost and support research engagement, and provide a fertile environment for research engagement to grow. The most elaborated example is the implementation of a research centre, a semi-autonomous organisation within the school which organises and supports the development of research activities. However, it's also possible for schools to demotivate their teacher-researchers via excessive managerialism and the use of short-term rewards.

Over the long term, the main factors which contribute to intrinsic motivation are a sense of community, the belief that their engagement with research is freely chosen, and a developing sense of competence in their own skills such as can be learned from working with peers with a high degree of expertise.

Further reading

Like it or not, a school is a complex social structure, and it helps to be able to navigate it successfully. 'The networked teacher: How new teachers build social networks for professional support' by Kira J. Baker-Doyle (2011, Teachers College Press) is a useful guide aimed especially at probationers and early-career teachers.

Discussion questions

- What would you put onto the reading list of a research reading group?
- What is the best way, in your experience, of engaging with a teacher who says very clearly and strongly, 'research is not for me'?

- What should be the role of school/trust/local authority management in a research centre? Is it best for it to be teacher-led, or could that present practical problems?

- What role should a research centre have in funding and staffing decisions? Should teachers who are closely involved in the research centre be allocated some time off timetable? Should the school recruit an expert teacher-researcher to lead the centre?

- What if a school has more than one group of research-active teachers, each of which wants to form its own research centre? Could a school have more than one research centre?

Notes

1 Robin Macpherson, deputy rector of Dollar Academy in Scotland and co-author of 'What does this look like in the classroom?' has done exactly this with multiple education authors, including a discussion of my own book, 'Psychology in the classroom'.
2 Lave, J. (1991). Situating learning in communities of practice. In L. B. Resnick, J. M. Levine, and S. D. Teasley (Eds.), *Perspectives on socially shared cognition* (pp. 63–82) (p. 65). Washington, DC: American Psychological Association.
3 p. 415 of Sachs, J. (2016). Teacher professionalism: why are we still talking about it?. *Teachers and Teaching*, 22(4), 413–425.
4 Ryan, R. M., and Deci, E. L. (2000). Self-determination theory and the facilitation of intrinsic motivation, social development, and well-being. *American Psychologist*, 55, 68–78.
5 Buehler, R., Griffin, D., and Ross, M. (1994). Exploring the "planning fallacy": Why people underestimate their task completion times. *Journal of Personality and Social Psychology*, 67, 366–381.
6 A free personality test is available online at https://openpsychometrics.org/tests/IPIP-BFFM

16 | Local networks

A great deal can be accomplished by trying to establish and carry out research within the walls of your school, but before long you may wish to focus your attention more widely. External researchers—teachers in other schools, universities or colleges and professionals in other relevant organisations—can be essential contacts, with a range of skills and expertise that no single school can possess by itself. Partnerships with such peers can be mutually beneficial.

This chapter looks at ways that local groups can be established, and at how to make them function effectively.

Benefits of partnership

Why would a partnership be useful to you? Just as teacher-researchers within a school can share ideas and collaborate on areas where they have complementary skills, extending this beyond the school further increases the pool of people with whom you can make links and engage in mutually beneficial sharing of research expertise. Such links can provide much-needed support to those who could otherwise feel isolated, especially those in small schools or in places where research engagement is just starting to take off.

A partnership or a broader multi-school network can also provide a break from the hierarchical nature of any school. Teachers at other schools don't owe you anything, you can't outrank each other and nobody is in charge, so any collaboration that takes place is strictly peer-to-peer.

Partnerships also extend the reach and impact of your work. After all, each separate organisation brings with it its own set of stakeholders and external contacts, providing new fora for sharing research outcomes. Contributing to successful cross-institutional research networks can help ensure that your research gets a chance to become more widely known. Even just the fact that you have formed a partnership or network makes your endeavours more noteworthy.

A partnership could also bring with it the opportunity to broaden and extend a current or recent research project. For example, let's imagine that you have conducted a study that is based around motivation in the classroom. Even a small-scale partnership between two schools could allow you to extend this work by looking to see whether the findings can be replicated in a different setting. If they can, this increases the chances that they apply more widely, making any intervention look more interesting and attractive to external organisations and funders. A simple but useful approach to start with, then, would be for each school to attempt to replicate recent work of the other.

On a larger scale, a multi-school network and/or one involving organisations in other sectors helps to expand the scale of any work. Each additional organisation that is added to the network brings certain logistical demands (can you all meet at the same time, for example? What about travel time and costs?) but also widens the pool of co-researchers and the number of potential study participants (a study on A-Level students across a whole city could have much more impact than a study of a single class in your school).

Establishing a local group

You may already be aware of teacher-researchers at other schools within your city or local area. If not, perhaps you can find out via social networks such as Twitter (a site that is very popular with research-engaged teachers), or by attending an event organised by the Chartered College of Teaching, ResearchEd, BERA or some other relevant organisation.

Failing this, you could consider ways of trying to encourage others to link up and join your current project(s). It should be easy enough to make contact with the other local schools—what about offering to go in and give a talk to their staff about your experiences and the research engagement that your school has been working on?

The very fact that you are reading this book shows that you have an understanding of the value of research, and are aware of issues such as maximising impact, reducing bias and managing workload. Perhaps you can attempt to make the same arguments to local colleagues.

Links with a university

The Higher Education sector is another excellent option for forming a research partnership. Universities have a built-in incentive to collaborate, due to requirements on them (via the REF, the research excellence framework) to demonstrate the impact of their work, and they will therefore love the chance to share their work with schools. They are also motivated to attract new students, and to raise the profile of their institution.

Again, if you do not already have contacts at the local institutions, this could be established without too much difficulty. Perhaps someone else at your school has a friend or spouse there? It can be surprising what a whole-staff email can uncover! Alternatively, most people who have been involved in mentoring student teachers (or have themselves recently gone through initial teacher education or forms of study) will have relevant contacts.

Other options for establishing links include:

- Arranging for a researcher in residence to come to your school.
- Volunteering on university summer schools or research projects.
- Corresponding with researchers whose work you admire.
- Attending conferences.
- Inviting scientists to give talks to your school.

All of the options above are beneficial in their own right, so the possibility of contacts with whom you could collaborate in future is really just a bonus.

Case study: a school-university collaboration

Schools and universities often collaborate, but this can be rather a top-down process, with university academics in the role of 'experts', telling teachers what and how to engage with research. This case describes a more grass-roots approach:

> In 2017, the Scottish Government released a research strategy which stressed the need for "increasing the levels of collaboration and communication between all actors within the education system".[1] In this context, one Scottish teacher decided to set up a school and university partnership in order to run a series of research projects.
>
> Staff from three schools and two universities joined the group. Membership was based on existing contacts through previous teaching and study. The group met first at one of the universities, but as time went on, meetings were also hosted by the schools. From the start, both university and school researchers were treated as equal partners.
>
> Given the group's interest in how teachers engage with research, they decided to conduct their first project into this very issue—how do schools make evidence-based decisions?
>
> As time went on, new members joined the group—but others left, due to time pressures, family commitments and so forth. As the group had no designated leader, this led to problems with re-allocating duties.

The case shows several interesting characteristics about how school-university partnerships can work. One of the most notable points is that it was initiated by a school teacher, leading to a greater sense of ownership than would happen if teachers were recruited to help with an existing university project. The variation of meeting locations and collectively planned aims of the group added to this sense of shared ownership.

(continued)

(continued)

It also led to a fairly egalitarian structure, but one which lacked clear leadership. Would it have been better if a single person had been in charge? Again, there would be drawbacks to putting university staff in control, but on the other hand, such academics have experience which might have been helpful when guiding the group.

One option might be to run such a group like a committee, with a chair and vice-chair. Each year the vice-chair can take over from the chair, with a new vice-chair being elected. This allows continuity, but also change. Such a structure could be designed to alternate the role of chair between university and school-based group, while also allowing less experienced members a year in which they essentially shadow the group's leader.

Events

An event can be one of the best ways of launching a network. Regular events and conferences can also help to maintain motivation among a school's research-engaged staff, keeping the issue at the forefront of their minds. Running an annual conference needn't be too demanding of time, especially if built into a local area's professional learning programme. The organisation of such an event could also be one role of a school research centre (see previous chapter).

A conference would also be a great way to formalise the sharing of research outcomes from collaborative projects or replications of each other's work, of the type already discussed. These could constitute the keynote talk, supplemented by findings of new original teacher-research in each partner school, along with short talks or posters presenting works in progress by other staff. Alternatively, a shared project could be provided as an introduction or a theme for the day, with keynotes from visiting researchers.

Depending on the size of the event, it may be necessary to take submissions from potential speakers and presenters. This is standard for most larger conferences—though you may also decide to invite certain speakers directly. Some may require a fee, though most research conferences keep costs to a minimum by not paying speakers (the assumed quid-pro-quo is that they are gaining the opportunity to share their findings, thus working towards their outreach targets). Travel costs should be budgeted for, however.

Pupils could also attend and benefit from the event, and pupils' own research could be shared at a research conference, particularly if it was innovative and unique (see Chapter 13). The local media may also be interested, especially at an inaugural event and one which involves pupil-researchers. How much more meaningful and motivating would it be for a budding researcher to share their findings not just with their own class but at a city-wide research conference, perhaps with the press invited?

From the research

Key issue: does leadership matter? The importance of leadership is much discussed in education these days, with certain headteachers lauded by government if they are perceived as having turned a failing school around. But does the evidence really support the idea that the characteristics and actions of an individual at the top can fundamentally change outcomes?

What the research says: there is a lot of research interest in leadership, although it is an area where it can be very difficult to establish the facts. This is in part because every leader is unique, and it's hard to know which of their various characteristics and skills have led to success (or otherwise). In addition, leaders change on the job as they gain experience, and (as all humans do) they behave slightly differently when in different settings.

In the realm of social psychology, numerous classic studies such as the 'Stanford prison experiment'[2] showed that people will change their behaviour and adapt to group norms

(continued)

(continued)

and expectations. However, the validity of such studies has been criticised—researcher Steven Reicher and colleagues have argued that the researchers of those studies inadvertently led participants to behave in particular ways.[3] It was their role as leaders which (accidentally) led to the dramatic behaviour change. A leader can set the tone for a group, either directly or implicitly indicating expectations and permissions.

According to psychology researcher Ronald Riggio, the characteristics that lead to gaining a leadership role differ from those that make someone successful if they actually become a leader. Drawing on the example of Donald Trump, Riggio notes that authoritarian leaders tend to be pushy, manipulative, oversensitive to criticism and harsh towards their subordinates. This tends to divide teams, with a core of enthusiastic followers forming while many others become discontented. In contrast, according to Riggio, more successful leaders are intelligent, hard-working, honest and compassionate.[4] None of these are personality characteristics, suggesting that (with the possible exception of intelligence) aspects of good leadership are practices that can be developed and strategically applied. Adding to this idea, Alex Haslam and colleagues have suggested that the key to successful leadership is not a trait at all, but instead lies in how well a person represents the values of the group as a whole.[5]

It's worth remembering that leadership is not just a feature of people in management positions. When defined in terms of having a vision, being influential and guiding people towards a shared goal, it encapsulates characteristics that could be shown by any member of staff. A head of department/faculty is a leader, while the classroom teacher is a leader of learning in the classroom, guiding their pupils towards educational goals. They may also be a leader in the professional network related to their subject area or their local research group.

Formalising a network

After a research network has been operating for a year or so, you may wish to establish a more formal identity and relationship, with a name, constitution and the like. This could be done on two main levels:

- Practitioners only: here the group maintains a peer-to-peer basis. You may have an organisational name, events and even a budget, but the senior management of the partner organisations have little or no involvement, and there is no formal or legal partnership. This type of network might best be conceptualised as a project.
- Strategic partnership: here, the organisations recognise the benefits of a partnership, and those working at a higher level draw up a formal agreement or memorandum of understanding. It could include a statement of mutual benefits, such as a university providing discounted courses or support to partner schools which work with it on research.

A practitioner-led group identity can help a research network to more easily communicate its goals, and encourage members to fully buy in (thus helping to sustain the work over time), but may suffer from a lack of ongoing commitment due to being an informal collaboration. Strategic partnerships can help to bring significant practical benefits, but may be associated with a loss of control on the part of the researchers themselves.

Either level is therefore potentially beneficial, but it would be best to wait until everyone involved is clear about the pros and cons, rather than rushing into new arrangements.

Research project: any research project could be inspired by this chapter's theme simply by conducting research which involves a co-researcher from outside your own institution. Often the topics

(continued)

(continued)

for such projects come from discussions at conferences or events, when shared interests become apparent.

If you have not already established such links, why not survey the rest of the staff in your school about the links that they already have with HE institutions and other educational organisations? Such information could prove extremely useful when forming a local group or planning an event.

How to do it: the first step for such a project would be to form a simple questionnaire which will ask about the organisations with which they have contacts. Ideally this will be answered by each member of staff, though it would also work if done on a departmental basis. From the point of view of confidentiality—and certainly if findings were going to be distributed or published in any form—information would need to be kept secure, with participants reassured that names and specific contacts would not be published. It is usually a good idea to specify example organisations (name specific universities, local authorities, government departments, local schools, and so on), and you may choose to focus on particular university departments, such as education, psychology, neuroscience or sociology.

The data from the questionnaire can then be analysed using **social network analysis**. This is a visual data analysis technique, popular in sociology, whereby people or groups are portrayed as nodes/circles on a diagram, and the ties between them as lines connecting the nodes. It results in a useful, easy-to-interpret visualisation of how well integrated the connections are in an organisation, and between organisations.

Imagine, for example, that a social network analysis of your school showed that the science faculty had ties with several universities, but that hardly any other departments did. This would show that the science teachers in the school would be a good starting place for building a local group that incorporated those outside organisations, and should therefore be encouraged to join (or to form their own research group). It might also cause you to question why this was the case, and what might be done to facilitate better networking by other departments around the school.

Concluding comments

Establishing a research network involving universities or other schools provides an ideal way to draw on expertise which complements your existing strengths. It is also motivating and enjoyable, helps to build an audience for your work, and can be the ideal stimulus to running research events that pupils can benefit from, too.

Overall, there is no doubt that running a large-scale research network provides something of a logistical challenge. Nevertheless, it should be remembered that each of the partner organisations will be conducting their own research and events, and the network should be mutually beneficial rather than burdensome. In the best cases, the partnership or network will provide much-needed support, and may even turn into a formal organisation in its own right.

Further reading

Although not aimed at teachers, 'The unnatural networker: How anyone can succeed at networking' by Charlie Lawson (2014, Panoma Press) is a useful book about how to go about forming and using contacts, particularly for those introverts to whom such skills do not come naturally.

Discussion questions

- Which teachers and departments in a school are most likely to have existing contacts with universities? Who is most likely to find it easy to establish such links?

- What are the advantages to the university of a link-up with a school? Consider availability of younger research participants, dissemination of their work, recruitment of future students, etc.

- What regular, ongoing activities could a partnership involve in your setting? Consider the provision of training, internships, hosting conferences, guest teacher/lecture posts, guest seminars, joint features in institution publications, etc.

Notes

1 https://www.gov.scot/publications/research-strategy-scottish-education/
2 Haney, C., Banks, W. C., and Zimbardo, P. G. (1973). A study of prisoners and guards in a simulated prison. *Naval Research Reviews*, 9, 1–17.
3 Reicher, S, Haslam, S. A., and Van Bavel, J. J. (2018). Time to change the story. *The Psychologist*, 31(8), 2–3.
4 Riggio, R. E. (2018). Leadership lessons from Donald Trump: How should a President lead? *Psychology Today*. Retrieved 28 January 2019 from https://www.psychologytoday.com/intl/blog/cutting-edge-leadership/201810/leadership-lessons-donald-trump
5 Haslam, S. A., Reicher, S. D., and Platow, M. J. (2010). *The new psychology of leadership: Identity, influence, power*. London: Routledge.

Disseminating your research

Applying research can be a great way of improving classroom practice and developing your professionalism. Conducting research, on your own or in a team, can help to develop your scientific understanding of teaching and learning in a way that benefits your practice. However, each of these processes is rather insular if you don't share the knowledge more widely. We will now consider how a teacher-researcher can become a champion of research, and use their skills and knowledge as a foundation to share ideas and make a wider impact.

One way of sharing research-based ideas is to publish your work. Many teachers assume that publication is only for university academics, but there are some teachers who publish prolifically. We will therefore look at how to identify and engage with academic journals as well as other suitable outlets for your work.

Case study: the new teacher

It might seem obvious that an experienced teacher who already has a lot of research experience can attract interest in their research work. But what about a teacher who is just starting out—will anyone pay attention to what they have to say?

(continued)

(continued)

Emma was in her NQT year working in a primary school in the north of England when she began to get involved with educational research. Her initial interest was sparked by work she had looked at during her initial teacher education, in particular the research evidence into engaging learners and helping them to remember more.

Emma focused her attention on PSHE, as she had mixed feelings about the accuracy of what was being taught in her school. She perceived that they took an over-simplistic approach to mental health by emphasising the role of stress, and largely ignoring unique individual or cultural thought processes or genetic explanations. She also felt that pupils didn't pay much attention to these lessons, and quickly forgot what they had been told.

To improve the quality of what was taught, Emma drew on examples of evidence-based mental health education in other countries. She found out that in some school systems, pupils are expected to understand theories and know research evidence rather than learning a set of tips and generalisations. Emma wrote a series of 'learning journeys' relating to anxiety and resilience. When she got feedback from a clinical psychologist that the lessons should cover more than just anxiety, she added additional extension lessons that explored stress-related psychosis, sensory processing issues, genetic factors in eating disorders, and the effect of mental health on concentration and memory.

To address class motivation in the learning of this material, she felt that forming the PSHE curriculum into a form of qualification with a whole-school assessment and certificate would be a good idea and could also help pupils to remember the information better, as it would be consolidated by studying for the assessment.

As part of the lessons, pupils developed the skills to investigate the effects of social media on mental health, using quantitative research methods and secondary data. Part of the plan was that teachers with expertise in survey-based research would guide this part of the course.

Emma's integrated, theory-based approach to teaching mental health attracted a lot of interest. She submitted proposals to local conferences, and soon found herself being invited to speak at national events. This brought her into regular contact with experienced and influential educators, and she was also a stalwart of online live chats about pupil well-being. Emma began a blog, which shared her particular perspective on these issues, as well as summarising recent research and sharing free resources.

What can be seen from Emma's case is that her relative lack of experience didn't restrict her enthusiasm for research or stop her making valuable connections. She thought widely about an issue that she was passionate about, making use of her understanding of memory and learning from her training, and also recognising a need in her new teaching context. Rather than relying entirely on her experience (which was limited), she drew on expert connections and found out about good practice in other countries. This led to opportunities to speak at conferences and otherwise share her ideas—people are always interested in hearing about something innovative, especially if it provides a model that could solve their own problems.

Internal publications and talks

Your own school's publications provide perhaps the most obvious and immediate way of sharing your research activities with other like-minded people, and yet are often overlooked. The people who read these are teaching in the same context as you, and will share many of your concerns. You don't need to take time to explain who you are, and the broader agenda (for example a school push on literacy) might already be a given. Options might include an email bulletin to staff, a newsletter to parents or any other way that information is shared in your context. Parents will be particularly interested to hear about projects that involve pupils (see Chapter 13). Wall displays could also be considered, either in the staffroom or corridors. If you are part of a local authority or a chain of schools, there may be opportunities to share among partner schools, too.

It's understandable if it feels intimidating to share within your own context—there can be a fear of being judged, and perhaps a sense that you are trying to look superior. One way to tackle and hopefully minimise this feeling is to present any research project as tentative and open to feedback, with an emphasis on the problems that you have faced in the classroom which stimulated the work. A poster which presents your research as a work in progress might also help to make the process of research engagement seem less intimidating to peers.

Don't underestimate how much colleagues will fail to understand or remember the details of what you are doing. You may find that colleagues are vaguely aware of 'some research thing' going on, and little more. In many cases, the details will be forgotten unless colleagues happen to speak regularly to the people involved.

Sharing research at conferences

As mentioned in the case study of Emma (see p. 238), it is never too early to get involved in conferences and events, and to seek out opportunities to speak, run a workshop or display a research poster. There are a great many events running every year. Some of the main options to consider are:

- Teachmeet
- ResearchEd
- Events run by your own subject-based teacher organisation
- Events run by teacher organisations such as Chartered College of Teaching.

While funding can of course be an issue, many of these are very cheap to attend, and tend to be timed to avoid school days, meaning that permission to attend is not an issue (though teachers with caring responsibilities will still face barriers).

If you are unsure about what events might be going on (it's easy to miss them, if you don't know what you're looking for), try asking around on social media. Most event organisers would be absolutely delighted at the prospect of an enthusiastic new delegate.

It can be well worth attending at least one event simply to observe, as gauging the level and style of the talks/presentations will make it easier for you to prepare a future presentation of your own.

If you look around and find that there are no local conferences, why not start your own? It doesn't need to be large scale in the first instance, and could constitute little more than a gathering of like-minded individuals that you are already in contact with (see the previous chapter). You could try one of the following formats:

- Unconference: how often have you been to a conference or CPD day and found that chatting to fellow delegates over coffee was more useful than the actual sessions? An 'unconference' tries to make the most of this feature by allocating more time to communication and sharing rather than lectures and workshops.

- Speed-geeking: this type of event takes a 'speed dating' format. For example, if you have eight speaker/presenters (pupil-researchers perhaps, as well as teacher-researchers), you would divide the audience into eight roughly equal groups labelled by number or a colour code, and each speaker could have a place (like the stalls in a traditional school fair or information evening). On a certain note (bell, tone, or just shouting 'time',) the group rotates round to the next speaker/presenter. This can be sandwiched in between other events such as a couple of keynote talks.

- Pecha kucha: these are short (20 slides in 6 minutes) powerpoint-based presentations. Again the emphasis is on allowing multiple speakers to share; making them so short allows for many more perspectives than is typical. A key tip is to avoid information overload

241

by keeping text on the slides to a minimum (done badly, a pecha kucha can resemble a 30-minute talk done at high speed!).

Blogging

Since the rise of blogging, many teachers have turned to the format as a way of sharing information and of getting feedback on their developing thoughts about teaching and learning. A blog (based on the term 'web log') is just a website for sharing text (and usually an image or two) about. . . Well, anything. Each 'post' can be an update on the same issue, or can be an entirely new topic—essentially like a short, self-produced online article. A blog post can be a great way to share information about research that you have engaged with, or a research project that you have been working on yourself.

Social media can then be used to share blog posts. When building up a presence on a social media platform, it is worth keeping in mind the interests of those you connect with. One hundred followers who share your interests and perhaps teach the same subject and age group can be more valuable for disseminating your ideas than a thousand more generic followers. Note that certain social media sites like Twitter and Instagram are sometime referred to as 'micro-blogging', as they present a quick and easy way to share very short texts online, alongside images and videos.

From the research

Key issue: can a committed teacher-researcher actually make a difference? Through sharing ideas on blogs and at events, is it possible that our passion will start to spread to others? Or will teacher-researchers forever be viewed as outsiders, or even marginalised in the general life of the school?

What the research says: the traditional view of *social influence* in psychology (and perhaps the obvious, common-sense position) is that a majority influences a minority. In the classic conformity research by Solomon Asch, students were asked to compare the lengths of different lines. The trick was that the other people in the room were actors, primed to give the wrong answer on certain occasions. The study found high levels of conformity—three quarters of participants followed the group and gave a blatantly wrong answer at least once.[1]

However, Asch's study also showed high levels of resilience under certain circumstances, such as when there was at least one other person who gave the correct answer. Researchers Elizabeth Lage and Serge Moscovici later argued that a minority can have a more lasting influence than a majority. A minority might not force people to comply immediately, but it is persuasive as long as it appears competent, assured and attractive.[2] Real-world examples of how a consistent, committed minority can influence a broader group include the suffragettes and the environmental movement—groups that were initially small, radical and on the margins of society, but whose message (women's right to vote and the need for eco-friendly action respectively) gradually came to be seen as the norm.

The hopeful conclusion that can be drawn from this is that as a committed and consistent voice in favour of teacher-research engagement, you can make a difference to broader attitudes throughout education.

Publishing a research article

The next step beyond (or as well as) the blog is to publish in a print or online journal edited by someone else. This presents a new challenge—someone will scrutinise and critique your work, and may reject it altogether. But the advantage is that publishing really makes you think about the quality and relevance of what you are sharing, hones your writing and greatly increases its impact. If an editor accepts it, then it's likely to be of interest to others, too.

The natural first choice for a teacher-researcher to consider may not be an academic journal, but rather the professional press—teaching or education magazines. These will often print research findings, and are also likely to be interested in reflections of how you have applied research in practice.

Moving on to academic journals, these print research articles subject to peer review (review by anonymous experts, as discussed in Chapter 3). The subject matter of such journals is new scholarship, meaning an idea or finding that moves the research field forward in some way. What should you write about? The obvious choice would be to publish the findings of a new investigation, as described in earlier chapters, such as an experiment, survey, interview-based study or correlation. However, other things that may well be worthy of publication include:

- A reflection/case study of setting up a school research centre.
- One or more interviews with teachers who are engaged with research.
- A philosophical critique of an educational policy or course.
- An evidence-based recommendation for future school courses, programmes or teaching methods.

Identifying an appropriate journal

Many journals may seem out of reach due to the theoretical depth and statistical complexity that they expect in their submissions. But look around. There are literally thousands of academic journals. There are certainly some which will be interested in publishing a practitioner's work or reflection.

Some ways to narrow the search include:

- Looking for journals which specialise in teacher research.
- Looking for journals which have published similar studies in the past.
- Looking through the submission guidelines (these can usually be found on the journal's website).

- Looking at the list of editors, and finding out whether they share your research interests.

Once you have narrowed the search down to a small number of options, you will want to look in more detail at the kind of papers that the journal has published in the past, ideally reading multiple previous articles. You also need to make sure that they publish the precise type of article that you intend to submit—some only publish qualitative research, for example. If in doubt, an email query to the editor can be worth a try; you won't always get a detailed response but some are very helpful. Your contacts can also help you to find out about markets for your work—another useful function of a research network (see previous chapter).

Submission

When it comes to your actual submission, the process varies; some journals are happy with a word-processed draft being emailed as an attachment, but many require you to use their own online upload system. Again, the journal's website is the place to find this out. Many journals are published by a few high-profile publishers such as Elsevier and Taylor & Francis—this can make things easier, as these titles often have similar processes for submission, and you won't need to register with each one separately.

Note that when it comes to publishing an academic journal article, there is usually no payment to the journal, though a few open access titles have moved to a model of charging authors a fee, which is generally covered by their institution or research grant. There is also no payment or royalty to the author.

Submitting an abstract

In some cases you will not be expected to send your entire manuscript to a journal, just the title and an abstract. The title of your report is quite different from the title of an essay. It should express the nature of the study in terms of the variables (independent and dependent variables), as accurately as possible. It should read something like: 'The effect of (independent variable) on (dependent variable)', usually with some reference to the methodology used. For example, the title of a study which investigated whether reducing background noise would improve pupil behaviour could read:

> 'An experimental study into the effects of background noise on pupil behaviour'.

You will no doubt be familiar, by now, with research abstracts—the short summaries that appear at the beginning of research articles, and can generally be accessed for free even if the whole article is behind a paywall. An abstract allows a reader to see at a glance what a research article is about. If you are submitting one, it must clear, succinct and accurate—the reader(s) should be in no doubt what the study was about. For an empirical (data based study), the abstract should include:

- A short statement of the issue being investigated, mentioning key background such as the theory that the study was based upon.
- The research method used.
- Who the participants were, and how they were selected.
- Details of the key research variables, with a summary of the hypothesis.
- Summary of the key results and main conclusion.

If a previous piece of research is central to your study, it can be mentioned in the abstract.

A local research journal

If you have drawn a blank when looking for an appropriate journal to publish your work, why not consider launching one of your own? A do-it-yourself approach is sometimes necessary when trying something new, as you may have found when establishing a research centre or local network.

This approach may seem akin to vanity publishing, but it's worth bearing in mind two things:

- Most journals are not aimed at you. Their audience is primarily composed of university-based academics, and as such they are set up with this group in mind as potential contributors and audience.

- It is not unusual for academics to start a new journal if a particular research topic or type of methodology is not currently well served. Many researchers have launched online-only journals to focus on a niche area. Teacher-produced research could face a similar issue.

Research project: a project that would be of great relevance to the classroom as well as to the professional challenge of presenting at conferences would be to investigate what makes a good speech. This could be done using existing video clips (e.g. TED talks or other videos via YouTube), or by making recordings of one or two short presentations by teachers or pupils.

How to do it: there are multiple options from the research methods discussed earlier in this book. For example, one or more videos of speeches could be shown as the subject of a focus group to gauge their responses, or participants could be surveyed to ask how they reacted to various aspects of the presentation and content.

You could also run a correlation study, looking for a possible relationship between a feature of a video (for example, its length or the clarity of the language) and how it is rated by viewers.

A more experimental approach would be to compare two subtly different versions of the same video—for example, with or without background music. You could survey participants' preferences, but also test their recall of the information (perhaps after a delay). Follow-up studies could systematically explore different aspects of the presentations until you reach a formula that seems to work.

Concluding comments

This part of the book has looked at how the teacher-researcher can benefit from leaving their bubble and making contacts and connections in their school and beyond. This chapter in particular has presented the argument that if research is worth doing, it's worth sharing. Doing so doesn't detract from the benefit that you may get from implementing your ideas, but allows a great many other people to benefit from them as well.

Some of the ideas for sharing are predicated to an extent on the issues of research quality discussed in earlier chapters (especially Chapter 9). There it was argued that teacher-researchers need to adopt scientific standards, because if research is not done well or adequately controlled, then it would be best if you didn't act on the findings. Likewise, such research is of little use to anyone else! A well-controlled study in a unique context, on the other hand, could be of broad interest. You will probably find, as you explore the literature, that there are surprisingly few recent studies of your area of interest that were conducted on learners like your own. Your findings can make a real difference, and can inspire other teachers to engage with research, too.

Further reading

Many of the books recommended in previous chapters include sections on preparing research for publication. Another excellent source is 'The psychologist's companion: A guide to professional success for students, teachers, and researchers' (6th edition), by Robert Sternberg and Karin Sternberg (2016, Cambridge University Press). Although aimed particularly at psychologists, it has useful guidance for all stages for the research and publication process, most of which is relevant to education writing.

Discussion questions

- What is a higher priority—doing research or sharing the findings?
- What is your preferred format for a conference or CPD event?

- If you were to launch your own conference or journal (or a combination of the two), what would be the focus, and how would you market it to others?

- What conferences or events are happening in your area over the coming year? Use a search engine and Twitter to find out, and draw up a short list of options.

Notes

1 Asch, S. E. (1955). Opinions and social pressure. *Scientific American*, 193(5), 31–35.
2 Moscovici, S., and Lage, E. (1976). Studies in social influence III: Majority versus minority influence in a group. *European Journal of Social Psychology*, 6(2), 149–174.

Glossary

Causation a cause-and-effect link between two variables, such that a change in one variable causes a change in the other. This can be demonstrated in experiments, but not in correlation studies.

Co-variables the variables investigated in a correlation study.

Condition part of an experiment or RCT in which there is a particular level/value of the independent variable that is being studied.

Confirmation bias a cognitive bias; the tendency to focus more on and remember ideas that fit our assumptions.

Confounding variable a variable which is not kept constant, and instead affects one part of the experiment more than the other, making results impossible to interpret.

Correlation a statistical means of comparing the levels of two or more variables, in order to get an idea of how they rise or fall together.

Correlation co-efficient a number that indicates how strong a correlation is, and what direction it is in.

Data the information gathered in a research study, whether numerical or verbal.

Dependent variable (DV) the variable that is measured in a research study such as an experiment or RCT, and which data gathered are assumed to reflect. It is the 'effect' under investigation, where the independent variable is the 'cause'.

Desirable difficulties features such as spacing that slow down the rate of learning and increase errors, but are desirable because they increase the long-term effectiveness or efficiency of learning.

Double blind design a research design which aims to avoid bias by ensuring that neither the researcher nor the participant knows which condition of a study each participant has been allocated to.

Ethical code of conduct a set of rules or guidelines for best practice, set out to help ensure that research on human participants does not harm those participants or infringe on their rights.

Ethical review board a structure within an organisation which has responsibility for scrutinising proposed new research and monitoring ongoing projects in light of ethical codes of conduct, and to ensure that they do not pose undue risks of harm to the people for whom the organisation is responsible.

Extraneous variables outside variables that cause random error in results, such as minor background noise and variations between participants' ability level.

False negative incorrectly concluding that the independent variable has not affected the dependent variable.

False positive incorrectly concluding that the independent variable has affected the dependent variable.

Generalising identifying the findings of research on one particular group and applying the same conclusions to a different or broader group.

Good participant effect bias due to research participants trying their best on a task in order to please the researcher or due to being pro-social.

Independent variable (IV) the variable that is manipulated in a research study such as an experiment or RCT. It is the 'cause' under investigation, where the dependent variable is the 'effect'.

Informed consent an ethical principle of research, where participants agree to take part in the study in full knowledge of what is going to happen.

Inter-observer reliability the extent to which two observers who watch the same behaviour record similar sets of data.

Interaction where one IV affects another, leading to non-linear changes in DV scores.

Interleaving modifying the order of a set of tasks or examples, such that different types are mixed together and appear side by side or consecutively.

Learning styles the notion, widely held to be a myth, that people can be categorised as different types of learner, and that their learning is optimised by focusing on their preferred sensory modality (e.g. visual, auditory).

Likert scale a questionnaire format which shows verbal items, and asks people to respond to these on a (usually) 7-point scale from strongly agree to strongly disagree.

Metacognition thinking about thinking, or a learner's knowledge of their own knowledge.

Naturalistic observation conducting an observation of real life as it happens, without interfering.

Negative correlation the statistical relationship between two co-variables whereby an increase in one variable is associated with a decrease in the other.

Neuromyths supposedly neuroscience-based strategies which have been dismissed as myths by later research, for example learning styles, brain gym, and left- versus right-brained learners.

Nudge psychology a field of psychology which investigates behaviour change which is motivated by small changes such as increased convenience or personalisation, rather than rewards or punishments.

Observation a research method which involves watching research participants and recording their behaviour as it happens.

Observation schedule a list of behaviours referred to during an observation.

p-value a number used in statistics which is compared against a standard value to determine whether a finding is statistically significant.

Pilot study a small-scale investigation used to help develop methodology and better specify research variables, as the first stage of larger research project.

Planning fallacy a cognitive bias whereby people underestimate the time required to complete a task or project.

Positive correlation the statistical relationship between two co-variables whereby an increase in one variable is associated with an increase in the other.

Pre-testing effect an effect in cognitive psychology where questions prior to instruction boost later learning, even if the learner cannot answer these questions.

Questionnaire a list of questions, used in surveys and interview studies.

Randomised controlled trial (RCT) a particular type of experiment which randomly allocates participants (or classes or schools) to a control condition, and others to one or more experimental conditions.

Representativeness the extent to which the participants in a study (the sample) are similar to the target population as a whole.

Research hypothesis a statement that predicts what will happen as the result of a change, or of the relationship between two variables.

Research methods ways of gathering data, such as surveys and interviews.

Researcher effect research participants being affected by the presence of the person who is running a study.

Retrieval practice actively retrieving information from memory in order to help to consolidate memory and understanding.

Sample the people studied in a particular research project, i.e. the participants who have been 'sampled' (selected).

Scattergram a graph used to give an initial visual impression of the relationship between co-variables in a study that uses correlation.

School research centre a semi-autonomous unit within a school which has responsibility for overseeing, supporting and planning research activities.

Screw-you effect bias where participants make no effort on the task or deliberately undermine it because they know it's of no benefit to them.

Social desirability bias the social pressure to please the person who asks the question. This can be a flaw in some surveys and interview studies.

Social identity how a person defines themselves in terms of the social group(s) of which they are a member.

Social network analysis a visual data analysis technique whereby people or groups are portrayed as nodes/circles on a diagram, and the ties between them as lines connecting the nodes.

Spacing effect a desirable difficulty whereby increasing the time delay between learning and practice makes the learning more durable over the long term.

Stress a bodily reaction to events that exceed a person's ability to cope. Research ethics require that we minimise stress to participants.

Structured observation setting up a task for people to do, and then observing them as they do it.

Transcription converting spoken recordings into a written text for analysis.

Transfer the ability to apply existing skills or knowledge to a new domain.

Triangulation collecting data in several different ways and comparing the results, for example behavioural measurements and questionnaires. It can be more accurate/less susceptible to bias than data from a single source.

Variable an aspect of human behaviour or environmental conditions which can vary; one of the aspects under investigation in a research study (see independent variable; dependent variable, co-variables).

Index

All sections of this book are indexed, including the introduction and the glossary. Indexed information in notes has been kept to a minimum, but where necessary it is indexed with an 'n' plus the note number after its page reference, e.g. 111n2. Terms within the glossary are indexed with a 'g' after the page reference, e.g. 250g. Square brackets around a page reference indicate that the content is a boxed suggested research project, e.g. attendance [150–151].

Printed in Great Britain
by Amazon